PRINCIPALITIES
AND POWERS

PRINCIPALITIES AND POWERS

A STUDY IN PAULINE THEOLOGY

The Chancellor's Lectures for 1954
at Queen's University, Kingston
Ontario

BY

G. B. CAIRD

Professor of New Testament Language
and Literature at McGill University
and Principal of
United Theological College
Montreal

OXFORD
AT THE CLARENDON PRESS
1956

Oxford University Press, Amen House, London E.C.4

GLASGOW NEW YORK TORONTO MELBOURNE WELLINGTON
BOMBAY CALCUTTA MADRAS KARACHI CAPE TOWN IBADAN

———

PRINTED IN GREAT BRITAIN

Contents

Introduction

WHEN Falstaff sold his soul to the devil one Good Friday for a cup of Madeira and a cold capon's leg, his friend the prince remarked of him: 'Sir John stands to his word, the devil shall have his bargain; for he was never yet a breaker of proverbs, he will give the devil his due.' There was a long period during which the proverb about giving the devil his due suffered much neglect at the hands of scholars, theologians, and preachers. But of late one eminent writer after another has urged us to pay more serious attention to the spiritual underworld. For example, Gustaf Aulen has reminded us that the classical doctrine of the Atonement represented the death of Christ neither as a satisfaction paid to God nor as a moral influence on men, but as a victory over evil powers.[1] Paul Tillich has written at length on the subject of the demonic, which he defines as 'the perversion of the creative';[2] C. S. Lewis has given us vivid portrayals of the 'lowerarchy' at work and, in particular, of the demonic capacities of an omnicompetent science;[3] and in the biblical field J. S. Stewart[4] and

---

[1] *Christus Victor.*

[2] *The Interpretation of History*, pp. 77 ff. In his earlier works Tillich seems to imply that the demonic is the product of an abuse of human creativity, but more recently, in his reply to his critics (in *The Theology of Paul Tillich*, ed. C. W. Kegley and R. W. Bretall, p. 343) he admits the possibility that the powers of evil are personal agents.

[3] *The Screwtape Letters* and *That Hideous Strength.*

[4] 'On a Neglected Emphasis in New Testament Theology', *Scottish Journal of Theology*, iv (1951), pp. 292–301.

T. W. Manson[1] have appealed for a renewed interest in
the spiritual background to the ministry of Jesus. But to
the best of my knowledge this new movement has not yet
produced any detailed treatment of Paul's thought on
this subject. Since 1909, when Dibelius wrote *Die Geister-
welt im Glauben des Paulus*, the majority of works on Paul's
theology, and especially those written in English, have
either evaded this aspect of his teaching or have given it
the niggardly acknowledgement of a few pages.[2]

Yet the idea of sinister world powers and their subjugation by Christ is built into the very fabric of Paul's
thought, and some mention of them is found in every
epistle except Philemon. There is the Satan who is constantly frustrating Paul's missionary work.[3] There is the
mystery of lawlessness (τὸ μυστήριον τῆς ἀνομίας), which
Paul at one time believed to be on the point of open
rebellion against God.[4] There are the elemental spirits of
the world (τὰ στοιχεῖα τοῦ κόσμου), by which both Jew
and Gentile were held in bondage, and which appear to
have close links with the law on the one hand and with
astrology on the other.[5] There is the god of this age (ὁ
Θεὸς τοῦ αἰῶνος τούτου), who 'has blinded the minds of
the unbelieving, that they might not behold the light of

[1] 'Principalities and Powers: the Spiritual Background of the Work
of Jesus in the Synoptic Gospels', *Bulletin of the Studiorum Novi Testamenti
Societas*, 1952.

[2] Since this was written, two additions to the literature have appeared
which are worthy of mention, though they have not made me wish to
alter any of my conclusions. They are: R. Leivestad, *Christ the Conqueror*,
and G. H. C. Macgregor, 'Principalities and Powers: the Cosmic Background to St. Paul's Thought', *New Testament Studies*, i (1954), pp. 17–28.

[3] 1 Thess. ii. 18; 2 Cor. xii. 7.

[4] 2 Thess. ii. 7.

[5] Gal. iv. 3; Col. ii. 8, 20.

the gospel of the glory of Christ'.[1] There is the ruler of the authority of the air (ὁ ἄρχων τῆς ἐξουσίας τοῦ ἀέρος), who is also described as 'the spirit now at work among the sons of disobedience'.[2] There are the rulers of this age (οἱ ἄρχοντες τοῦ αἰῶνος τούτου), who crucified the Lord of Glory and thereby compassed their own downfall.[3] There are the principalities and authorities (αἱ ἀρχαὶ καὶ αἱ ἐξουσίαι), over which Christ celebrated his triumph on the Cross.[4] In spite of this defeat the world-rulers of this darkness (οἱ κοσμοκράτορες τοῦ σκότους τούτου) are still operative, and the Christian must wrestle with them;[5] they still hold the whole creation in bondage to futility, though they cannot separate the Christian from the love of God.[6] But the day must come when every principality and every authority and power (πᾶσα ἀρχὴ καὶ πᾶσα ἐξουσία καὶ δύναμις) will yield to Christ, since 'he must reign until he has put all his enemies under his feet'.[7] This, however, is not Paul's last word concerning the destiny of the powers, for he came to believe that they were created beings, created in and for Christ, whether thrones or lordships or principalities or authorities (εἴτε Θρόνοι εἴτε κυριότητες εἴτε ἀρχαὶ εἴτε ἐξουσίαι);[8] and that it was God's purpose that they should be reconciled to him by the blood of the Cross,[9] that angelic as well as human tongues should confess Jesus as Lord,[10] 'that to the

---

[1] 2 Cor. iv. 4.   [2] Eph. ii. 2.   [3] 1 Cor. ii. 6.   [4] Col. ii. 15.
[5] Eph. vi. 12.   [6] Rom. viii. 20 f., 38 f.   [7] 1 Cor. xv. 24.
[8] Col. i. 16; ii. 10.   [9] Col. i. 20.
[10] Phil. ii. 11. Many of the older commentaries on this verse leave us with the impression that ἐπουρανίων refers to unfallen angels. But there are two reasons for rejecting this interpretation. Elsewhere (Eph. ii. 2; vi. 12; cf. Slav. En. xxix. 5 and Charles's note) the heavens are represented as the abode of the spiritual forces of wickedness; and in the

principalities and authorities in the heavenly places there might now be made known through the church the manifold wisdom of God'.[1]

From this very rapid survey of a dozen or more passages from the epistles it is apparent that the concept of world powers reaches into every department of Paul's theology, and that it cannot be dismissed as a survival of primitive superstition. Paul is using mythological language, but his language has a rational content of thought; he is working with ideas which have had a long history, but he is describing spiritual realities with which he and his fellow Christians have personal acquaintance. When I say that Paul's language had a rational content I do not, however, mean that Paul or anyone else in the first century had developed a logical system of demonology. One of the difficulties of our theme is that the evidence does not fall into any neat pattern. Indeed, it is the nature of religious symbolism and myth that it can convey truths which defy the precision of analytical thought.

As we study Paul's teaching, we shall raise questions which carry us outside the scope of biblical scholarship. Does evil exist? Are there personal powers of evil? If so, what do we mean by 'personal'? Such questions as these I propose to leave to the philosopher. We shall also be inclined to ask how the message of the Bible on this subject is to be accommodated to modern categories of thought; but that is the function of systematic theology.

present passage Paul declares that Christ underwent the humiliation of the Cross and the subsequent exaltation in order to bring these heavenly beings, along with those on earth and those under the earth, into the subjection of faith.

[1] Eph. iii. 10.

Our present task is descriptive—an attempt to reconstruct something of the world of thought in which Paul's mind was at home. In any such research into the spirit of another age or another civilization it is comparatively easy to analyse, to unweave the rainbow of a man's thought into its constituent colours; but it is a far harder matter to detect those unconscious, unquestioned associations which enabled men's minds to move rapidly from one set of ideas to another. With this warning against the dangers of analysis I propose to analyse Paul's conception of principalities and powers into its component elements, always reminding myself that the strands of thought which I shall separate out never actually existed in separation.

In the first chapter, then, I shall examine the Jewish and Christian attitudes to the fact of pagan religion and pagan power. In the second chapter I shall try to show how Paul came to regard the law as a demonic agency. In the third chapter I shall discuss the biblical ideas concerning the irrational factor in the physical universe. And in the final chapter I shall endeavour to explain what Paul meant by saying that all these enemies had been vanquished by Christ.

I

The Rulers of this Age

I

FROM the time when the Israelites entered Canaan and came face to face with the elaborate nature worship which has been so vividly illuminated for us by the Ras Shamra texts, they were almost continually confronted with the problem of foreign religion. What attitude was the worshipper of Yahweh to adopt towards pagan deities? There were three possible ways of resolving the religious conflict—syncretism, suppression, and subordination—and each of them was tried.

The first and most obvious method of procedure was to identify Yahweh with one or more of the Canaanite gods; with the supreme god El or with the younger and more vigorous Baal, who seems to have been supplanting El, much as Zeus in Greece supplanted Kronos.[1] There is ample evidence in the Old Testament that at one time this syncretism was generally accepted, and that it was abandoned only after centuries of protest from the prophets, who declared that the low moral standards encouraged by paganism were incompatible with the lofty demands of Yahweh. The prophets themselves would have preferred to suppress pagan worship altogether. From Elijah's vituperative ridiculing of Baal on Mount Carmel

[1] See A. S. Kapelrud, *Baal in the Ras Shamra Texts.*

there is an unbroken line of succession to Deutero-Isaiah's contemptuous dismissal of the Babylonian stocks and stones which had no spiritual reality behind them. But whatever might be said about pagan gods, pagan religion held an influence over human lives which could not be laughed out of existence. Accordingly, a third theory was developed, which existed for centuries alongside of the other two, but which eventually came to displace them both.

According to this third theory the beings whom other nations worshipped as gods were in fact subordinate powers acting under the supreme authority of Yahweh. These beings are known either as *Elim* and *Elohim* (i.e. gods) or as *bene Elim*, *bene Elohim*, and *bene Elyon* (i.e. sons of God).[1] First,[2] then, the superiority of Yahweh to the other gods is asserted.

> Who is like to thee, O Yahweh, among the gods?[3]

The inferior gods are called upon to recognize the supremacy of Yahweh.

> Give to Yahweh, O ye sons of God,
> Give to Yahweh glory and strength.[4]

[1] The Hebrew *ben* in these titles denotes not filial relationship but classification. In the same way the expression 'sons of the prophets' denotes a professional guild, whose members had not necessarily inherited their prophetic powers from their fathers. *Ben* is used frequently in Hebrew in descriptive phrases: a son of ninety years, i.e. ninety years old (Gen. xvii. 1); son of man, i.e. a human being (Ps. viii. 4); sons of exile, i.e. exiles (Ezra iv. 1); sons of death, i.e. men doomed to die (Ps. lxxix. 11).

[2] Much of the evidence that follows is drawn from the Psalms, which are notoriously difficult to date. I do not suggest that the passages cited occur in their chronological order, but simply that they illustrate the logical steps in the development of this doctrine.

[3] Exod. xv. 11.   [4] Ps. xxix. 1.

These supernatural beings are conceived as forming a heavenly council around the throne of God.

> Who in the heavens can be compared to Yahweh?
> Who is like Yahweh among the sons of God,
> A God feared in the assembly of the holy ones,
> Great and terrible above all that are about him?[1]

Under this new heavenly régime the powers of nature were transformed into ministering angels of Yahweh,

> Who makest winds thy messengers,
> Fire and flame thy ministers.[2]

Among the nature spirits to be made subservient to the God of Israel were the Cherubim, who may possibly have come into Canaanite religion from the older cults of Babylonia, and who in later times were to become second among the hierarchies of heaven.

> He rode upon a cherub and flew,
> He came swiftly upon the wings of the wind.[3]

It has been suggested that this development began during the period of the Judges, and provides the explanation of the title 'Yahweh of hosts', which first came into use at that time.[4] Yahweh, as God of the angelic hosts, exercised control over the powers of nature. Whatever may have been the truth of its origin, this is certainly what the title came to mean to readers of later times, and it may be that Amos already understood the phrase in this light, for he uses it in a description of Yahweh as Lord of nature.

---

[1] Ps. lxxxix. 6–7. [2] Ps. civ. 4. [3] Ps. xviii. 10.
[4] V. Maag, 'Jahwäs Heerscharen', *Festschrift für Ludwig Köhler, Schweizerischen Theologischen Umschau* (1950), pp. 27–55; but see also I Sam. xvii. 45.

For lo, he who forms the mountains and creates the wind,
And declares to man what is his thought,
Who makes the morning darkness, and treads on the high
    places of the earth—
Yahweh, God of hosts is his name.[1]

The stars, too, were included in Yahweh's angelic retinue; for Israel had regarded them as animate beings at least as early as the time of Deborah, when

> From heaven fought the stars,
> From their courses they fought against Sisera.[2]

In the Old Testament 'the host of heaven' usually denotes the sun, moon, and stars; but sometimes, by a studied ambiguity, it denotes also the heavenly court of Yahweh. Thus Micaiah ben Imlah declares to Ahab: 'I saw Yahweh sitting on his throne, and all the host of heaven standing by him on his right hand and on his left'.[3] The book of Job depicts for us in vivid terms the day of creation,

> When the morning stars sang together,
> And all the sons of God shouted for joy.[4]

Thus when Israel came into contact with the astral deities of the east, she was already prepared to accommodate them to her scheme of things. They were not gods in their own right but angelic viceroys with a delegated power.

II

By the time of the Exile this article of faith had been further elaborated by writers of the Deuteronomic school. In the poem of Deuteronomy xxxii we read:

[1] Amos iv. 13; cf. ix. 3 f.   [2] Jud. v. 20.
[3] 1 Kings xxii. 19; cf. Neh. ix. 6; Dan. viii. 9–11.
[4] Job xxxviii. 7.

When the Most High gave to the nations their inheritance,
When he separated the sons of men,
He fixed the borders of the peoples
According to the number of the sons of God.
For Yahweh's portion is his people;
Jacob is his allotted inheritance.[1]

Each nation, that is to say, has its own angelic ruler and guardian, except Israel, which comes under the direct sovereignty of God. The Deuteronomist does not seem to have been disturbed by the knowledge that the pagan nations worshipped their angelic rulers in the place of God. These rulers had been allotted to them by God and, provided that Israel was not seduced by their worship, the order of God's providence was not disturbed. 'Beware lest you lift up your eyes to heaven, and when you see the sun and the moon and the stars, the whole host of heaven, you are drawn away to worship them and serve them, which Yahweh your God has allotted to all the nations under the whole heaven.'[2] All the disasters which come upon Israel are to be attributed to this one cause, that 'they went and served other gods and worshipped them,

---

[1] Deut. xxxii. 8–9. In verse 8d the M.T. reads: 'according to the number of the sons of Israel'—a corruption of the text which could have arisen either through the use of an abbreviation for the divine name, or more probably because of the coincidence that Jacob's family at the time of the descent into Egypt numbered seventy (Exod. i. 5). When these lectures were prepared, the reading given above was a conjectural emendation, based on the LXX. It has since been confirmed by one of the Qumran texts—see P. W. Skehan, 'A Fragment of the "Song of Moses" (Deut. 32) from Qumran', *Bulletin of the American Schools of Oriental Research*, no. 136 (December 1954).

[2] Deut. iv. 19; cf. xvii. 2–7.

gods whom they knew not, and whom he had not given them'.[1]

These ideas were developed in the later Jewish writings. In the book of Daniel we read of a war between the prince of Greece and the prince of Persia.[2] But these princes are not to be identified with Alexander the Great and Darius III. They are the angelic guardians of the two nations; for in a later passage a third prince appears on the scene, whose name is Michael, the great prince who stands for the people of Israel.[3] In one of the Targums it is said that every nation has its own guardian angel who pleads before God the cause of the nation under his protection,[4] and we shall see in the next chapter that Michael came to be regarded as Israel's defending counsel in the heavenly law-court. The late Hebrew Testament of Naphtali has a quaint contribution of its own.

For at that time the Lord, blessed be he, came down from his highest heavens and brought down with him seventy ministering angels, Michael at their head. He commanded them to teach the seventy families which sprang from the loins of Noah seventy languages. Forthwith the angels descended and did according to the command of their Creator. But the holy language, the Hebrew language, remained only in the house of Shem and Eber, and in the house of Abraham our father who is one of their descendants.[5]

The Deuteronomic doctrine had three strong points in its favour. In the first place, it did justice to the reality of pagan religion and of the pagan political power with

---

[1] Deut. xxix. 26; cf. Sir. xvii. 17.   [2] Dan. x. 13, 20.
[3] Dan. xii. 1.   [4] Ps.-Jon. on Gen. xi. 7 f.
[5] Test. App. 1. viii. 4–6 (R. H. Charles, *Apocrypha and Pseudepigrapha*, ii, p. 363).

which religion was inseparably associated. It was a common phenomenon in the ancient world for a deity to be the personification of the state over which he presided; and, under the successive domination of Babylon, Persia, Greece, and Rome, Israel was to have ample opportunity to discover that the pagan empires, whether they were symbolized by their earthly kings or by their heavenly guardians, constituted a power to be reckoned with. In the second place, the Deuteronomic teaching asserted that all authority, by whomsoever it is exercised, comes ultimately from the one God. Without some such teaching it would have been all too easy for the pious Israelite to assume that the Gentile nations lay totally outside the sphere of God's kingly rule. In essence, therefore, the belief in national angels was a courageous proclamation of the universal sovereignty of God. It is true that Old Testament theology always recognized the existence of a demonic fringe, where, as we shall see in the third chapter, the writ of Yahweh did not run; and, when Israel came to ever-closer grips with the mystery of iniquity, there was a tendency to enlarge this fringe, and to project the sovereignty of God into an eschatological future. But throughout all the developments that followed, it is important for us to remember that the Jews never really doubted that Gentile authority was derived from the Lord of all majesty and might, and that their pagan oppressors had no power over them except what was given them from above. In the third place, Deuteronomy preserved the distinction between two modes of divine sovereignty. Israel had voluntarily accepted Yahweh as king, and had undertaken to obey his laws; over her he could maintain a direct and personal rule. Where his rule was unknown and his authority unacknowledged, his control, though none the less real, was necessarily indirect and impersonal. Even in its most broad-minded moments the Old Testament provides no support for the belief that one religion is as good as another.

III

During the centuries that followed Israel lived almost continuously under the sway of one world empire after another, and it did not take her long to discover that the providential order, as expounded in Deuteronomy, had become deeply corrupted. Her pagan neighbours appeared to her to be tyrannical, immoral, and superstitious; and if the earthly kingdoms were tainted with evil, the angelic rulers could hardly be acquitted of responsibility for sins committed under their supervision. This theme is strikingly illustrated by Psalm lxxxii, which pictures God standing in the heavenly court, accusing his heavenly entourage of acquiescing in human injustice, and threatening them with death in spite of their divine nature.

> God stands in the divine council;[1]
> He judges among the gods;
> 'How long will you judge unjustly,
> And show partiality to the wicked?' . . .

[1] This is the R.S.V. translation, and is the best that can be done with the M.T. But the LXX reads 'in the council of the gods' (ἐν συναγωγῇ θεῶν), which gives a better parallelism and is probably the correct reading.

> I say, 'Though you are gods
> And sons of Elyon all of you,
> Yet you shall die like men
> And fall like one of the princes'.

The theory generally put forward to explain this corruption of earth and heaven was that idolatry is the root of all evil. God had set the heavenly bodies in the sky to mark out the seasons, and had given to his angels authority over the nations. Men had made the mistake of offering to the creature the worship which is due only to the Creator. This is one of the leitmotives of that cycle of psalms (xciii, xcv–xcix) which is associated with the enthronement of Yahweh.

> A great God is Yahweh
> And a great King above all gods . . .
> The sea is his and he made it,
> And his hands formed the dry land . . .
> Great is Yahweh, and greatly to be praised;
> He is to be feared above all gods.
> For all the gods of the nations are idols,
> But Yahweh made the heavens . . .
> All who worship images are put to shame,
> Who boast in their idols;
> All gods bow down before him . . .
> For thou, O Yahweh, art most high over all the earth;
> Thou art exalted far above all gods.[1]

Men had exalted that which was secondary and derivative into a position of absolute worth, and by accepting their worship the rulers had become involved in their sin. It is important to notice, however, that there is no question at this stage of any precosmic fall of the angels, such

[1] Ps. xcv. 3, 5; xcvi. 4–5; xcvii. 7, 9.

as we find in some of the later Jewish literature.[1] The corruption of the heavenly order is the result of human sin.

But the Hebrew mind was less interested in the origin of evil than in its conquest. The apocalyptic writings abound in assurances that the pagan empires, along with their angelic rulers, are doomed to final defeat.

And it shall come to pass in that day that Yahweh will punish
The host of the height in the height
And the kings of the earth on the earth.[2]

Yahweh is exasperated with all nations
And furious with all their hosts;
He has devoted them to destruction,
He has given them over to the slaughter . . .
And the heavens shall roll up like a scroll;
And their host shall fall
As leaves from a vine,
As they fall from a fig tree.[3]

In these two passages there is a parallelism between the earthly kingdom and the angelic ruler; both are in rebellion against Yahweh and both are to be brought under the final judgement.

These two quotations help us to understand one of the commonest elements in the apocalyptic writings—the cosmic catastrophe in which the stars drop from their courses and the heavenly bodies withdraw their light. The symbolism by which this idea is expressed undoubtedly owes something to the belief that the New Exodus, in which God would visit and redeem his people, must follow the pattern of the first Exodus, and be

[1] e.g. Slav. En. xxix. 4 ff.   [2] Isa. xxiv. 12.
[3] Isa. xxxiv. 2, 4.

heralded by disasters similar to the plagues of Egypt. As the plagues signified the eclipse of Egyptian power by the superior power of Yahweh, so the eschatological disasters represented in the minds of the apocalyptic writers the ultimate defeat of those spiritual powers which underlay the pagan world order.

The classic expression of this hope is found in the book of Daniel. The four beasts of Daniel's vision, representing the successive empires of Babylon, Media, Persia, and Greece, reach the climax of their atrocities when the 'little horn' of the fourth beast makes war against the saints and introduces into the temple the 'desecrating horror'.[1] Then the judgement throne is erected and world dominion passes to 'one like to a son of man', the symbolic representative of Israel.

IV

Before we pursue these lines of thought into the New Testament, we must turn aside for a moment to look at the evidence of the Septuagint. For it is here that we find the terms powers (δυνάμεις), authorities (ἐξουσίαι), principalities (ἀρχαί), and rulers (ἄρχοντες) applied for the first time to angelic beings. Where the Hebrew speaks of God's hosts, the Greek sometimes speaks instead of his powers.

> Praise him, all his angels;
> Praise him, all his hosts (LXX: all his powers).[2]

> Praise the Lord, all his hosts (LXX: all his powers),
> His ministers who do his will.[3]

[1] Dan. vii. 21 ; xi. 31.   [2] Ps. cxlviii. 2.
[3] Ps. cii (ciii). 21 ; cf. Isa. xxxiv. 4.

'Εξουσίαι and ἀρχαί occur in the two alternative versions of Daniel vii. 27 : 'all authorities (principalities) shall serve and obey him.' And the angelic princes of Persia, Greece, and Israel mentioned later in the book of Daniel become ἄρχοντες, the rulers of this age.[1]

Particular interest attaches to the Greek renderings of the title 'Yahweh of hosts'. The translator of Isaiah merely transliterated, thereby making Sabaoth into a proper name. But in the Psalter we find ὁ Κύριος τῶν δυνάμεων—Lord of the powers; and in the prophetic corpus this rendering occurs along with another, ὁ Παντοκράτωρ—the Omnipotent. Of these two renderings the one is a translation, the other an accurate paraphrase. For God's omnipotence is to be seen precisely in his lordship over the cosmic powers.

In one passage, where the Hebrew text denounces the heathen gods as idols, the Septuagint has substituted the word δαιμόνια—demons.[2] We must be careful here not to read too much into the Greek word. To us the word demon tends to call up a mental picture of a little black man with horns, barbed tail, and toasting fork, but to the Greeks it denoted any heavenly mediator between God and man.[3] Plato had spoken of δαιμόνια as guardians of cities,[4] so that they filled in his philosophy the same place as the angelic rulers occupied in Jewish theology. Nevertheless, in hellenistic Judaism the term came to be used in a bad sense,[5] although there was no reason in Greek

---

[1] Dan. x. 13, 21; xii. 1.   [2] Ps. xcv (xcvi). 5.

[3] Plato, *Symp.* 202E; πᾶν τὸ δαιμόνιον μεταξύ ἐστι θεοῦ τε καὶ θνητοῦ.

[4] *Leg.* iv. 713C ff.; v. 738D.

[5] Deut. xxxii. 17; Ps. xc (xci). 6; cv (cvi). 37; Isa. xiii. 14; xxxiv. 14; lxv. 3, 11; Bar. iv. 7, 35.

usage why the word should not have conveyed the same qualified approval that Jewish thought extended to the guardians of the nations. In this connexion we must note also the distinction drawn in the Wisdom of Solomon between two aspects of pagan religion. The author regards the worship of the heavenly bodies as misguided but pardonable, whereas 'the devising of idols was the beginning of fornication, and the invention of them the corruption of life'—a statement which is illustrated by a grim catalogue of pagan vice.[1]

Echoes of the Septuagint vocabulary are to be found in the intertestamental literature. In the book of Enoch we read of 'sun, moon, and stars, and all the powers of heaven which revolve in their circular chariots'. Another passage predicts that God 'will summon all the host of the heavens, and all the holy ones above . . . and all the angels of power, and all the angels of principalities, and the Elect One, and the other powers on the earth and over the water'. Yet another section of the book promises that the seventy angelic shepherds of the flock of God, having abused their God-given authority, will eventually be brought under judgement.[2]

The terminology of the Septuagint may well have been deliberately chosen to provide a bridge between Hebrew and Greek thought. The Stoics had used the term δυνάμεις to designate the immanent 'qualities' of their pantheistic universe.[3] In his creation myth in the *Timaeus* Plato had spoken of the stars as 'visible and created gods', who

---

[1] Wisd. xiii–xiv.
[2] 1 En. lxxxii. 8; lxi. 10; lxxxix. 59 ff.; xci. 15.
[3] Diog. Laert. vii. 134, 147.

derived their divinity from the one God, the Demiourge.[1]
Aristotle, too, believed in the existence of one God,
the Prime Mover, but did not hesitate to speak of the
stars as 'divine bodies'.[2] No educated Greek, therefore,
would be at all disconcerted by a foreign philosophy
in which the gods of the Greek pantheon were reduced
to the rank of powers, acting under the authority of
one supreme God. Moreover astrology, an invader from
the east which had made an almost complete conquest
of the Greek mind, had taught men to believe that
their lives were controlled in every part by astral influences, the elemental spirits of the universe.[3] Following the example of the Babylonians, the Greeks had
identified the planets with the five principal gods in
the pantheon—Hermes, Aphrodite, Ares, Zeus, and
Kronos—and these are the names which in their
Roman guise the planets bear among us to this day.
These astral gods were known to their worshippers as
ἄρχοντες.

The doctrine of divine powers which we find in the
writings of Philo of Alexandria is a magnificent hybrid of
the Hebrew and the Greek. Philo believed that the two
creation stories of Genesis i and ii described two distinct
acts of creation: the first was the creation of an intelligible
world, corresponding to Plato's world of ideas; the second
was the reproduction of this ideal pattern in the material
universe. Philo uses the word 'powers', without any
attempt at consistency, to denote one of three things:
sometimes they are attributes of God, sometimes they are

---

[1] *Tim.* 40D.   [2] *De Cael.* 292ᵇ33.
[3] See F. Cumont, *Astrology and Religion among the Greeks and Romans.*

created beings identical with the Platonic ideas,[1] and some-times, again, as in Stoicism, they are immanent causes in the material world,[2] though Philo censures the Stoics for imagining that such powers could be corporeal and in-dependent of any higher cause. In their third capacity the powers are occasionally to be identified with angels.[3] According to Philo God performs some of his providential actions directly and personally, and others through the agency of incorporeal powers.[4] These powers are divided into two classes: those which perform the functions of government and punishment, and those which mediate God's goodness, e.g. the beneficent powers of nature.[5] Or, to put it in another way, primary benefits come directly from God; secondary benefits[6] and punishments belong to the created order, which, though it derives its existence from God, operates with some degree of independence.

With the intricacies of Philo's exegesis we are not imme-diately concerned, for they have little bearing on the theology of Paul. But it is interesting to note that a hel-lenistic Jew, reading the Scriptures in the Septuagint version, took the title 'Lord of the powers' to mean that God's providence functions for the most part through a system of powers, including those which are responsible for government.

V

Paul, too, was a hellenistic Jew, and his intellectual back-ground helps us to understand his attitude to the Roman

---

[1] *Spec. Leg.* i. 13; *Monarch,* i. 6; *Opif.* 4–5; *Sacr.* 13.
[2] *Spec. Leg.* iii. 34; *Migr.* 32; *Immut.* 8; *Conf.* 13.   [3] *Abr.* 28.
[4] *Mut.* 8.   [5] *Sacr.* 15; *Cher.* 9; *Legat.* 1; *Qu. in Exod.* ii. 68.
[6] *Leg. All.* iii. 62.

Empire. In the face of the evidence which I have presented there can be little doubt that his 'principalities and powers' included the powers of state; though we shall find that he greatly enlarged the conception of the powers so as to include the Jewish religion, and indeed the whole natural order, under the demonic reign which the Jews had seen at work in the Gentile world.

How deeply Paul was imbued with the Jewish idea of angelic powers behind the pagan world order may be seen from three passages in 1 Corinthians. In each case the reference to these powers is incidental to the main argument, as though their existence was taken for granted and no further explanation was necessary. The first of these allusions occurs when Paul is administering a rebuke to the intellectual snobs of Corinth and remarks in passing that he is always ready to discuss theology with those who have the necessary religious qualifications.

We do speak wisdom among the mature, but a wisdom not of this age nor of the rulers of this age who are being reduced to impotence. Rather do we speak a secret wisdom of God, the hidden wisdom which God foreordained before the ages for our glory; which none of the rulers of this age knew; for if they had known it, they would not have crucified the Lord of glory.[1]

This passage must be interpreted in the light of 1 Corinthians xv. 24, where it is obvious that the principalities, authorities, and powers which are being reduced to impotence by the regnant Christ are spiritual beings.

[1] 1 Cor. ii. 6–8.

Behind Pilate, Herod, and Caiaphas, behind the Roman state and the Jewish religion of which these men were the earthly representatives, Paul discerned the existence of angelic rulers who shared with their human agents the responsibility for the crucifixion.

A little later in the same epistle Paul rebukes the Corinthians again for carrying their personal quarrels into the public law-courts. This, he declares, is to reverse the proper order of things, inasmuch as the saints are destined to share with Christ his function of world judgement. Those who are to judge the world should not allow the world to judge them. Surely even the humblest Christian is competent to act as judge in matters of daily life. 'Do you not know that we are to judge angels?'[1] Here the context makes it plain that the angels of whom Paul is thinking are those who supervise the secular state, including the administration of justice.

The third mention of angels is a notorious *crux interpretum*. The church of Corinth had written to Paul to ask for his authoritative opinion on a variety of perplexing subjects, and amongst other questions they had asked how far Christians, with their new sense of freedom in the Gospel, were to be bound by the conventions which governed the behaviour of women in Greek society. In the course of his reply Paul asserts, almost in parenthesis, that 'a woman ought to have an authority (i.e. a veil) on her head because of the angels; nevertheless in the Lord woman is not independent of man nor man of woman'.[2] The natural assumption is that the angels here are the same as those already mentioned in vi. 3, and this

[1] 1 Cor. vi. 3.   [2] 1 Cor. xi. 10 f.

interpretation not only gives excellent sense but gains strong confirmation from the contrast which is drawn in these two verses between conduct which is made necessary because of the angels and conduct which is made possible in the Lord. For Paul believed that the Christian was living at one and the same time in two ages and under two régimes. In the new Christian society the old social inequalities had been superseded, and the only proper relation between husband and wife was interdependence. 'There is neither Jew nor Greek, there is neither slave nor free, there is neither male nor female; for you are all one in Christ Jesus.'[1] But though Christians by faith were already living in the new age and in the new creation, they were also still living in the old order, and a respectful acceptance of its laws and customs, in so far as this was compatible with their new Christian loyalty, was still part of their obedience to God. The subjection of woman to man, like the subjection of slave to master, was part of the structure of the pagan social system, and any Christians who ignored that system would be undermining the divinely decreed order of natural law whereby the present age was governed. Therefore out of deference to the angelic guardians of the natural order of society, Christian wives ought not to appear in public without a veil, the symbol of their subjection to their husbands.

Unfortunately the meaning and the forcefulness of this argument have been obscured by their context. For in the preceding and succeeding remarks Paul tries by an appeal first to Scripture and then to Nature to give his instructions a universal validity which was quite out of keeping

[1] Gal. iii. 28.

with his considered opinion. His case may be para-
phrased as follows. Man is the image of God: he was
made to reflect the divine glory and in particular the
divine authority. If man refuses to exercise this delegated
authority over the rest of creation, he brings dishonour
upon himself and upon the God for whose glory he was
created. By putting upon his head a veil, the symbol of
subjection, he dishonours not only the head which is
thus covered but also the Head who is the source of his
authority and for whose honour he ought to live. Woman,
on the other hand, was created not for authority but for
subjection. Her life was derived from man's, was created
for his sake, and should be lived to his glory. Indeed, she
is his glory if she accepts his authority over her and its
symbol, the veil. By discarding the veil, and with it her
true womanhood, she brings dishonour to the head of
her body and also to the head of her life, her husband.
Similarly, long hair is shameful in a man and a cropped
head is shameful for a woman. Thus a man who wears
his hair short and uncovered accepts his rightful place of
authority and honours God; and a woman who wears her
hair long and veiled accepts her place of subjection and
honours her husband. Nor is this doctrine based only on
the word of Scripture, for it is a lesson which Nature herself teaches by providing woman with long hair as a
natural covering.

This is Paul at his worst. He uses the word 'head' in
two senses at once, the one literal and the other meta-
phorical. His argument from Nature is no argument at
all; for, if Nature has supplied woman's head with a
natural covering, what need is there to add an artificial

one? But a much more serious fault is that the whole argument depends on a misquotation of Scripture, and one which might have been pardonable in English, but which is without excuse in Greek. In English the one word 'man' has to do double service for the human race as a whole and for the male members of the species. Hebrew, Greek, and Latin all have two words: *'adham*, ἄνθρωπος, and *homo* mean 'a human being, irrespective of sex'; and *'ish*, ἀνήρ, and *vir* mean 'a male person'. Now in Genesis i. 27 it is written: 'God created man (*'adham*) in his own image, in the image of God he created him; male and female he created them.' It is not man the male but man the human being who was made in the image of God, so that the whole Scriptural argument for the subjection of women falls to the ground.

It would be possible to contend that, in spite of its faulty logic and equally faulty exegesis, this passage nevertheless represents the sincere belief of Paul that the subjection of woman to man was part of the Creator's intention. For in two later epistles he reiterates his instructions to Christian wives to submit to their husbands as a Christian duty.[1] If we adopt this line of reasoning, then we must conclude that the angels of 1 Corinthians xi. 10 are simply the guardians of the created order, without any suggestion that they may be at variance with the true purpose of God. But there are several reasons which should give us pause. The instructions to wives in Colossians and Ephesians are part of a 'code of subordination' which the early church adapted from pagan sources, with the addition of Christian

[1] Col. iii. 18; Eph. v. 22–33.

motives.[1] The code includes a command to slaves to obey
their masters, and it can hardly be supposed that Paul
or any other Christian believed slavery to be part of the
purpose of the Creator. The purpose of the code was to
impress upon converts the necessity of respectful submission to the established order of society, even where
that order appeared to them to be contrary to God's
purpose as revealed in Christ. It is true that in Ephesians
Paul gives Christian reasons for the submission of wife to
husband, but these reasons have the effect of transforming
the whole relationship. For the wife is to submit not to her
husband's authority but to his self-sacrificing love, so that
the fusion of their two persons becomes a sacramental
replica of the mutual indwelling of Christ and his church.
Moreover, we have to reckon with the two explicit state-
ments of Paul that 'there is neither male nor female; for
you are all one in Christ Jesus'; and that 'in him all things
were created'.[2] Taken together these two sayings can
only mean that the equality and interdependence of the
sexes which have been made possible in the order of
redemption were intended by God in the order of creation.
For all these reasons it seems best to infer that in 1 Corinthians xi Paul is being inconsistent and is refusing to
accept the logic of his own position.

It has been necessary to expose the insufficiency of
Paul's spurious arguments for the veiling of women in
order that we may the better appreciate the strength of
his one sound argument. The subjection of women did
not rest on God's eternal purpose in creation, but it was

[1] See Weidinger, *Die Haustafeln*; Carrington, *The Primitive Christian Catechism*. [2] Gal. iii. 28; Col. i. 16.

part of the structure of ancient society; and Paul believed that that society was controlled by angelic rulers who, though corrupt and doomed to lose their power, retained as long as the present age lasted the stamp of their original God-given authority.

VI

We are now in a position to discuss another passage which has given rise to prolonged controversy.

Let every person be subject to the supreme authorities (ἐξουσίαις ὑπερεχούσαις). For no authority exists except by the will of God, and those that exist have been instituted by God. So that he who resists authority resists God's institution; and resisters will incur judgement. For rulers (ἄρχοντες) are not a terror to good conduct but to bad. Do you wish to escape fear of an authority? Do good and you will receive his approval; for he is God's minister for your good. But if you do wrong, be afraid; for he does not bear the sword in vain. For he is God's minister, executing the retribution of his wrath on the wrong-doer.[1]

There is no doubt that Paul is here thinking of personal agents who represent the Roman state, but are those agents of angelic powers or of human officials? Ἐξουσία, like its Latin counterpart *potestas*, can mean either public office or, occasionally, those who held such office, the authorities;[2] and an example of this usage in the second sense is found in Luke xii. 11. On the other hand, in every other place where Paul uses ἐξουσία in the plural he is referring to the angelic authorities. Perhaps Cull-

---

[1] Rom. xiii. 1–5.

[2] See W. Forster in *Kittel's Theologisches Wörterbuch zum N.T.* ii, p. 560; and for *potestas* see Lewis and Short.

mann is right in claiming that Paul had both interpreta-
tions in mind, and deliberately used terms which could be
taken either way.[1] We have already seen that pagan
nations could be represented either by their angelic
governors or by their earthly rulers, either by 'the host
of the height' or by 'the kings of the earth'. There was,
therefore, no reason why Paul, in urging Christians to
obey the Roman state, should not be allowed a certain
ambiguity of expression. By the same token it is unnecessary for the expositor of Paul to commit himself at
this point, for neither the exegesis of the present passage
nor Paul's theology as a whole will be fundamentally
affected by our answer to this question. Paul's belief in
angelic beings who stand behind the political institutions
of paganism is too well attested in other passages to be in
dispute; so that, even if this idea was not in the forefront
of his mind when he wrote Romans xiii, it would still be
quite legitimate to use what he says there about the
Roman state to throw light upon his conception of
principalities and powers, and also to interpret Romans
xiii in the light of that larger conception.

Some commentators have been perplexed by this passage because they have felt that Paul was ascribing to the
state the right to demand absolute obedience, and that
this was hardly compatible with Paul's own supreme
religious loyalty to Christ. But, in fact, Paul inherited
from his Jewish forebears a very different doctrine: that
the angelic guardians of pagan nations exercise a delegated authority, and that any derivative authority which
sets itself up as an absolute authority, demanding absolute

[1] *Christ and Time*, pp. 195 f.

obedience, takes on a demonic character. In the next chapter we shall see that there is a good parallel between the authority of the pagan state and that of the Jewish law; for the law was also a divine institution, but it too had only a secondary authority, and when men tried to make its authority absolute they made it demonic.[1] Paul's teaching in Romans is entirely in harmony with this general background. For he does not say that the state embodies the whole authority of God; it had been created for a single specific purpose, to maintain order and to suppress crime. As long as the state continues to perform its God-given task, even if in other respects it shares in the general corruption of the present world order, it still possesses a divine authority which the Christian must obey, not merely from fear of the consequences but also 'for conscience sake'. In other words, it is a Christian duty to keep within the law and to refrain from any conduct which will weaken the fabric of society.

At this point a word must be said about Cullmann's interpretation of Romans xiii. He holds that Paul's instructions to the church in Rome to obey the powers of state were related to his belief that by the Cross those powers had already been made subject to Christ. 'Paul starts from the principle that the State has attained to such a dignity that obedience is due to it, not by reason of its original nature, but only because it has been given its place in the divine order [sc. the order of redemption].'[2] Without discussing what was the original nature of the state before it was given its place in the divine order he

---

[1] See also H. M. Gale, 'Paul's View of the State', *Interpretation*, vi (1952), pp. 409–14. [2] Op. cit., p. 200.

goes on to assert that this order is the kingly rule of Christ. 'State and church both belong in the kingdom of Christ, and yet not in the same way, since only the church knows it, while the state, in so far as it is a pagan state, does not know it.'[1] Before the coming of Christ the angelic powers of the pagan state exercised a divine authority only because 'they were destined to be subjected through Christ'.[2] The significance of this argument becomes apparent when we concentrate not on what Cullmann is affirming but on what he is denying. For he is denying that the creative activity of God has any meaning apart from his redemptive activity in Christ, and that the New Testament teaches a belief in natural law.

It is no service to the apostle Paul to father upon him a deficient doctrine of creation. The things which Cullmann denies are precisely the things which Paul affirms. The powers of state are to be obeyed not because they have been made subject to Christ but simply because they exist, and because no authority can exist apart from God's decree. Their authority belongs not to the order of redemption but to the order of creation. Paul achieves the universal centrality of Christ not by making the authority of the powers depend on the Cross but by declaring that Christ is God's agent in creation. 'In him all things were created in heaven and on earth, visible and invisible, whether thrones or lordships or principalities or authorities.'[3] It is only by keeping a clear distinction between the two divine orders that we can avoid the inconsistencies of Cullmann's theory, in which the state, though it belongs to the eternal kingdom of Christ's redemption, still

---

[1] Ibid., p. 204.   [2] Ibid., p. 210.   [3] Col. i. 16.

continues to act as a demonic power and is doomed ultimately to pass away. For whatever Paul believed about
the divine authority of the state, there can be no doubt
that he believed also in its demonic capacity; and for a
description of the Roman state in its dual aspect we must
turn now to an even more obscure passage in an earlier
letter.

VII

In the year A.D. 40 the emperor Caligula gave orders that
his statue should be set up in the temple at Jerusalem.
Early in the following year he was assassinated, before his
instruction had been carried out, and his order became
a dead letter; but in the interim the shock of his action
reverberated through the Jewish world. The Jews felt
that in Caligula the pagan world order had reached the
climax of its antagonism to the sovereignty of God: this
was the 'desecrating horror' prophesied by Daniel as the
immediate precursor of the Judgement. Ten years later,
when Paul wrote to the church of Thessalonica, these
ideas were still running in his mind.[1] The Parousia of
Christ, he declares, will not happen until after the Rebellion. There is at work in the world a 'mystery of lawlessness', which has shown its colours in the person of
Caligula, and which will shortly break out in open revolt
against God, when 'the man of sin . . . takes his seat in
the temple of God, setting himself up as God'. But this is
not the whole truth about the Roman Empire. Besides the
mystery of lawlessness there is at work also a 'restraining
power' ($\delta \kappa \alpha \tau \acute{\epsilon} \chi \omega \nu$); Caligula has been removed, and all

[1] 2 Thess. ii. 1–10.

that he stood for is for the moment held in restraint. The restraining power can only be Rome in the exercise of her God-given function of government. Thus does Paul in a single passage delineate the ambiguous nature of Roman power. From one point of view the state was fulfilling its divinely appointed office of restraining the evil-doer, but from another point of view its authority was so corrupt as to be constantly in danger of usurping the authority of God.

In the following year Paul was brought before Gallio and received a first-hand impression of the impartiality of Roman justice; and this was not the last occasion on which he was to owe either life or liberty to the intervention of Roman officials. As his appreciation of Roman law deepened, his memories of Caligula faded, so that when he wrote to the church in Rome he could speak of the divine authorization of the Roman state without any mention of its demonic possibilities. This mellowing of Paul's attitude towards Rome goes some little way to explain another change which took place in his thinking at about the same time. In his earlier writings Paul accepted the apocalyptic outlook, which did not look beyond the defeat of those spiritual powers which were at enmity with God. They belonged to the present age, and with the passing of the present age they too would pass away. But in his imprisonment epistles he has begun to entertain the hope that even the powers may be brought within the scope of God's redemption. God had exalted Christ 'that at the name of Jesus every knee should bow, of those in heaven and those on earth and those under the earth, and that every tongue should confess that Jesus Christ is Lord.'[1] The heavenly powers are among those who must come to acknowledge the lordship of Christ, for it was to this end that they were created. Christ is 'the firstborn of all creation, because in him all things were created in heaven and on earth, visible and invisible, whether thrones or lordships or principalities or authorities . . . in him all the fulness of God was pleased to dwell, and through him to reconcile to himself all things, whether on earth or in heaven, making peace by the blood of his cross'.[2] Nor is this some far-off, divine event, to take place in the twinkling of an eye, at the last trumpet: it is happening now. For it is God's purpose 'that to the principalities and authorities in the heavenly places there might now be made known through the church the manifold wisdom of God'.[3] Like the redemption of the Christian, the redemption of the powers is achieved by the Cross, worked out in the present, and consummated at the Parousia.

This final development was a most important addition to Paul's doctrine of the state. The passages from 1 Corinthians and Romans which we have examined give little encouragement to Christian social action. They draw a clear-cut distinction between state and church, the one being the sphere of law and the other the sphere of grace. Christians live in two worlds, and, although in the Lord they have entered into a new freedom, they are not entitled to use that freedom to break down any of the social and political institutions of the old order in which they still live. It would seem to follow from this that the Christian must accept the authority of the state, not

[1] Phil. ii. 10 f.   [2] Col. i. 16, 20.   [3] Eph. iii. 10.

seeking in any way to influence or alter its policies, in the confidence that the state belongs to the present age which is already passing away. It is, of course, open to the modern theologian who dislikes this attitude to the state to point out that the early church, as a small minority movement in the Roman Empire without any hope of being able to affect the affairs of state, could hardly adopt any other course, and that Paul's teaching therefore is not of universal validity. But such a protest is unnecessary, for Paul's belief in the redemption of the powers opens up possibilities far beyond the range of what was practicable in his own day. If the angelic beings who preside over the pagan world order are capable of being reconciled to God, does not this require us to believe that institutions such as the state, in which human sin is organized in what Tillich has called 'a structure of evil', are also capable of redemption?

This redemption of the powers must not be confused with Cullmann's idea that through the Cross the state has, without knowing it, been brought within the kingdom of Christ. For Paul declares that the powers must confess that Christ is Lord, and that, through the mediation of the church, they must come to understand the wisdom of God's redemptive purpose. There is a helpful parallel here between the individual and the corporate redemption. Men and angels alike have been reconciled to God through the Cross, but in each case the redemptive act of God must be accepted by faith, worked out in a life of obedience to Christ, and brought to completion at his Parousia.

Most theologians would agree that the state derives its

authority from God, that it is subject to demonic corruption, but that it can still provide a framework of law and order within which the gospel of man's redemption may be preached; and there they would stop. Indeed, there is an influential school of modern theology which asserts that the Christian is so deeply involved in the sinfulness of the social order that he may not at any point contract out of it, that any attempt to practise the ethical teaching of Christ is sheer hypocrisy, and that Christian ethics must always be the ethics of compromise. In remarkable contrast to this modern pessimism, Paul seems to me to say that the Christian's loyalty to society and the state, which are derivative authorities, must always be subordinated to his loyalty to the absolute authority of God in Christ; and that by the continued influence of Christ, working through his loyal followers in the church, the state itself may be brought progressively more and more within the Christian dispensation, and the affairs of state directed not merely by the ethics of law but by the ethics of the Gospel.

II

The Great Accuser

I

THERE is general agreement that Satan is a fallen
angel, but there is a difference of opinion as to the
date of his fall. One school of thought, of which
John Milton is the best-known English exponent, main-
tains that Satan's ejection from heaven occurred before
the creation of the world, and this belief can be traced
back to Jewish sources.[1] But in the main biblical tradition
the fall of Satan from heaven coincides with the ministry
of Jesus, and in particular with the Crucifixion.[2] Up to
that point Satan regularly appears in heaven and has
every right to be there.

The Hebrew word *satan* means 'adversary', and the
earliest use of the word as a theological term is illustrated
by the story of Balaam. When Balaam is on his way to
curse Israel, his passage is blocked by an angel of Yahweh, who says, 'I have come out as an adversary, because
your way is perverse before me'.[3] Whether we regard the
angel of Yahweh as an emissary of God or as a periphrasis
for God himself, the function of the *satan* is to oppose the
wrong-doer; and it is a divine function. Similarly, the
foreign kings sent against Solomon in the days of his

[1] e.g. Slav. En. xxix. 4 ff.
[2] Lk. x. 18; Jn. xii. 31; Rev. xii. 10.   [3] Num. xxii. 32.

apostasy are described as *satans*, that is, agents of the divine judgement.[1] In the prologue to the book of Job the task of withstanding evil-doers has devolved upon a single angel, who is accordingly known as the Satan. He is one of the sons of Elohim and has the right of access to the heavenly court. In that court he acts as public prosecutor;[2] his duty is to indict sinners before the bar of the divine justice. To that end he spends his time going to and fro in the earth and observing men (*Have you considered my servant Job?*), so that anything they say or do may be used in evidence against them. In the visions of Zechariah the Satan, as prosecutor, seems to have a better chance of success than he had in the case of Job. The high priest Joshua, the representative of the people of Israel, is brought into court wearing filthy garments, which symbolize the moral and religious condition of Jerusalem. But God orders the high priest to be clothed in clean raiment, and so by the redemptive intervention of God the Satan loses his case.[3]

The word *satan* occurs without an article for the first time in 1 Chronicles xxi. 1. Satan has now become a proper name. The passage describes how Satan incited David to take a census, an act for which he was subsequently punished by God. Now according to 2 Samuel xxiv. 1, it was God who incited David, in order that he might have a cause for punishing him. The chronicler, therefore, by his alteration of the text, has provided the first indication of a feeling, which was later to grow to

---

[1] 1 Kings xi. 14, 23.
[2] For the use of *satan* as a human prosecutor, see Ps. cix. 6.
[3] Zech. iii.

a conviction, that to God's servant Satan may be ascribed
activities which are unworthy of God himself, and that
Satan's work, though it is done in the name of God, is in
some way contrary to the real divine purpose.

But before we trace the development of this theme, let
it be noted that throughout the New Testament period
Satan retains his juridical duties. He is a legal adversary
(ὁ ἀντίδικος ὑμῶν) ;[1] those who are conceited fall victims
to his condemnation.[2] The book of Jude commends to its
readers the courtesy and restraint which Michael showed
towards Satan when the two of them were engaged in a
legal battle for the possession of the body of Moses.[3] In
the Revelation John sees a war in heaven between Michael
and Satan. Satan is cast out and a voice is heard saying,
'Now is come the salvation and the power and the kingdom of our God and the authority of his Christ: for the
accuser of our brethren is cast down, who accuses them
before our God day and night; and they have overcome
him because of the blood of the Lamb'.[4] As long as there
are sinners to be arraigned before the judgement seat of
God, there is work for Satan in heaven. But when Christ's
redeeming work is done, when, in the words of Paul,
'there is now no condemnation to those that are in Christ
Jesus',[5] then Satan can be relieved of his legal responsi-
bilities. It should be noted in passing, however, that
Satan does not relinquish his office without a struggle,
and this points to a contradiction in his nature which we
must investigate later.

[1] 1 Pet. v. 8.
[2] 1 Tim. iii. 6.
[3] Jud. 9.
[4] Rev. xii. 7-12.
[5] Rom. viii. 1.

In the Rabbinic writings, where the atoning work of
Christ is, of course, unacknowledged, Satan retains his
office as accuser.[1] The Midrash on Exodus xii. 29 tells us
that Michael and Sammael (another name for Satan) are
like the advocate and the accuser who stand before a
tribunal. Some ingenious person discovered that if you
give the Hebrew letters of Satan's name their numerical
value and add them up, the total is 364; and the moral
of that is that Satan has divine permission to act as accuser for 364 days in the year, but on the Day of Atonement the courts are not in session, and Satan must take
one day's compulsory holiday.[2]

In none of these passages is there any suggestion that
Satan abuses his office by false accusation or slander. It is
true that in the Septuagint the regular translation of
satan is ὁ διάβολος, and that this name is in the New Testament almost interchangeable with ὁ Σατανᾶς. But in
classical and hellenistic Greek διάβολος means either an
adversary or a slanderer, and it is obviously because of
the former meaning that the word was chosen by the
Septuagint translators as the equivalent of *satan*.[3] We
cannot, of course, rule out the possibility that a Greek
Christian would read into the word διάβολος something
of the second connotation, and this may have happened
in 1 Peter v. 8, where the legal hazards attendant on the
Christian profession arise for the most part out of the
false accusations enumerated in iv. 15. But in general it
must be said that, in so far as Satan is guilty of slander, it
is slander against God and not against man. In Bere-

---

[1] Berak. 46[a].   [2] Yom. 20[a]; cf. Midr. on Lev. xvi. 3.
[3] See W. Forster, *Kittel's Theologisches Wörterbuch zum N.T.* ii, pp. 69 f.

shith xx. 1 he is identified with the slanderer of Psalm
cxl. 12, because 'he uttered slander against his Creator'.
Similarly when Jesus in the Fourth Gospel accuses Satan
of lying, it is because he tells lies about God.[1]

II

Besides Satan the Old Testament knows of other law-
enforcement officers. There are the angels of punishment
and the angel of death. At first punishment and death
were considered to be inflicted by the angel of Yahweh—
a periphrasis for Yahweh himself.

> Let them be as chaff before the wind:
> And let the angel of Yahweh chase them.
> Let their way be dark and slippery:
> And let the angel of Yahweh persecute them.[2]

'And it came to pass that night that the angel of Yahweh
went out and smote in the camp of the Assyrians a
hundred and eighty five thousand.'[3] But what began as
a periphrasis developed into a being or beings dis-
tinguishable from Yahweh.

> His soul draws near to the grave,
> And his life to the destroyers.[4]

> He cast upon them the fierceness of his anger,
> Wrath and indignation and distress,
> A mission of angels of punishment (lit. evils).[5]

---

[1] Jn. viii. 44–47. The argument of this passage runs as follows: The
devil was a murderer from the beginning, brought death to Adam and
Eve, because he had not the truth about God and therefore told lies
about him. The Jews are his children, because they do not know the
truth about God and so cannot recognize that truth when it is spoken to
them by Jesus and embodied in his life. That is why they want to mur-
der him.   [2] Ps. xxxv. 5–6.

[3] 2 Kings xix. 35; cf. 2 Sam. xxiv. 16.

[4] Job xxxiii. 22.   [5] Ps. lxxviii. 49.

For our study of Paul this last passage is of particular interest with its close association between angels and the wrath of God.

In the later literature there was a tendency for these punitive duties to be taken over by Satan. The Rabbinic writings often speak of Satan when nothing more than death is meant, as, for example, when it is said that Satan dances between the horns of a mad ox.[1] Paul speaks of handing a man over to Satan 'for the destruction of his flesh, that his spirit may be saved in the day of the Lord Jesus'.[2] In Hebrews Satan is 'the holder of the power of death',[3] and in Revelation he is the Destroyer, in Hebrew Abaddon and in Greek Apollyon.[4] But Satan also expanded the sphere of his influence in another direction. In the story of Job Satan was not only the accuser: he was also given permission to subject Job to a series of tests, to see whether he would commit any sin worthy of condemnation. From being the tester of men he became by an easy transition their tempter, as in 1 Chronicles xxi. 1. Thus to the original office of public prosecutor he added two others: that of *agent provocateur*, canvassing for business for the law-court, and that of executioner, carrying out the court's sentence. This enlargement of Satan's duties is explicitly described in Baba Bathra 16ᵃ: 'Satan comes down to earth and seduces, then ascends to heaven and awakens wrath; permission is granted to him and he takes away the soul . . . Satan, the evil impulse, and the angel of death are all one.' The same threefold function is ascribed in the book of Enoch not to one Satan but to

---

[1] Pes. 112ᵇ; Ned. 31ᵇ. [2] 1 Cor. v. 5.
[3] Heb. ii. 14. [4] Rev. ix. 11.

a group of angels who are called satans or angels of punishment; they tempt men to evil,[1] accuse the sinners before the Lord of spirits,[2] and execute punishment on the guilty.[3] Elsewhere in the same book it is said that these satans are under the authority of the one Satan, whose kingdom in turn is subject to the Lord of spirits.[4]

But can he who incites men to disobedience and then claims possession of them in the halls of death be regarded as a servant of God? Is he not rather the enemy of God? That is the role allotted to Satan in the gospels, where the whole ministry of Jesus is presented as a campaign between the kingdom of God and the kingdom of Satan. And that is the role which he has played ever since in Christian theology.

What, then, are we to make of this remarkable Rake's Progress, whereby Satan, the servant of God, entrusted with the maintenance of divine justice, becomes the Devil, the enemy of man and God. We cannot say that in the process he loses anything of his original character. Throughout his tragic history his zeal for justice remains unimpaired. He is a martinet, who demands that men shall be dealt with according to the rigour of the law, and will go to any lengths to secure a verdict. His tragedy consists precisely in this, that law is not the ultimate truth about God, so that, in defending the honour of God's law, Satan becomes the enemy of God's true purpose.

The decline of Satan was undoubtedly accelerated by extraneous causes. The influence of Persian dualism on

---

[1] En. lxix. 4 ff. In lxix. 1–3 these angels are confused with the fallen angels, but see Charles's note. [2] En. xl. 7.
[3] En. liii. 3; lvi. 1; lxii. 11; lxiii. 1. [4] En. liii. 3; lxv. 6.

Jewish thought is undeniable, and this must have accentuated the hostility between God and Satan. The identification of Satan with the serpent of Eden and with the dragon of the creation myth must have contributed to the same result.[1] But these developments were possible only because there was already a contradiction in the very nature of Satan.

Philo's treatment of this paradox may help to carry our argument a stage farther. In the first chapter I drew attention to Philo's belief that acts of Providence are of two kinds: those which come directly from God and those which come through the mediation of incorporeal powers, including beneficent powers on the one hand and regal or punitive powers on the other. In one passage he attempts to explain this distinction. 'There is only one God, but this one God has about him innumerable powers as helpers and saviours of all created existences. Among them are punitive powers. . . . The King [sc. God] communes with his powers, and uses them as his servants for the performance of such duties as are not appropriate to God himself.'[2] Philo seems to have felt that the enforcement of law and the punishment of sin, though they rest on a divine decree, are no adequate indication of the essential character of God. How little does he know of God who knows only the demand of the Lawgiver and the condemnation of the Judge!

For further illumination let us turn to John of Damascus.

The works of Providence are partly according to good will (κατ' εὐδοκίαν) and partly according to permission (κατὰ

[1] Wisd. ii. 24; Rev. xii. 9.　　　　　　　　　[2] *Conf.* 36.

συγχώρησιν). . . . Also one must bear in mind that God's original wish was that all should be saved and come to his kingdom. For it was not for punishment that he formed us but to share in his goodness, inasmuch as he is a good God. But inasmuch as he is a just God, his will is that sinners should suffer punishment. The first then is called God's antecedent will and pleasure, and springs from himself, while the second is called God's consequent will and permission, and has its origin in us.[1]

In the light of this analysis we can see more clearly the true character of Satan. God's consequent will and permission, we are told, has its origin in us. Because man has abused his freedom, God is compelled to make a response which is different from his eternal purpose of grace. What happens by God's consequent will or permission, the punishment of the sinner, is actually the frustration of God's antecedent will or purpose that all should be saved. Satan, then, who is the guardian of God's consequent will or permission, becomes the enemy of God's true purpose of grace, because he treats that which is secondary and relative to man's sin as if it were the absolute will of God.

III

Paul has a number of ways of expressing this demonic paradox. There is, first, the wrath of God. Paul is quite clear that the wrath which comes upon the children of disobedience is God's wrath. It is 'revealed from heaven against all ungodliness and unrighteousness'.[2] He believes in a 'day of wrath' for the impenitent, when 'for those who are perverse and do not obey the truth but obey

---

[1] *Fid. Orth.* ii. 29.   [2] Rom. i. 18; cf. Eph. v. 6.

unrighteousness, there will be wrath and fury'.[1] Yet he
will never speak of the wrath as though it were a personal
attribute of God. It works, rather, as an impersonal
principle of retribution. It comes inexorably on the sen-
sual.[2] It overtakes the wrong-doer through the police
action of the state.[3] In the Roman reprisals against their
nationalist outbreaks it had already come upon the Jews
to the uttermost.[4] But Paul does not believe that wrath
is the true purpose of the Creator. 'God has not destined
us for wrath but to obtain salvation through our Lord
Jesus Christ.'[5] Even when he is wrestling with the mystery
of Israel's rejection, which he felt so strongly because he
had played a leading part in bringing it about, although
he suggests that perhaps the divine Potter has formed
some vessels for wrath and some for mercy, this is not
his final word; for he comes to the conclusion that 'God
has shut up all men into disobedience that he might have
mercy upon all'.[6] The wrath is God's wrath, and yet it
is so far in conflict with God's eternal purpose of grace
that God has undertaken in Christ to deliver men from
his own wrath.[7]

Closely associated with the wrath is the law: 'for the
law brings about wrath.'[8] Like the wrath, the law is God's
law: it is 'the oracles of God', it is 'holy and just and good',
it is 'spiritual';[9] but it does not reveal the true and complete character of God. Against those Rabbis who asserted
that the Torah lay on the knees of God before the creation of the world Paul declares that the true nature of

[1] Rom. ii. 5, 8.   [2] Col. iii. 5.   [3] Rom. xiii. 4.
[4] 1 Thess. ii. 16.   [5] 1 Thess. v. 9.   [6] Rom. ix. 22 f.; xi. 32.
[7] Rom. v. 9; 1 Thess. i. 10.   [8] Rom. iv. 15.
[9] Rom. iii. 2; vii. 12, 14.

God was expressed in his promise, and that the law was a later addition made because of transgressions.[1] Or, in the language of John of Damascus, the promise contains God's antecedent will, which springs from himself; the law contains only his consequent will, which has its origin in man's sinfulness.

Provided that the law is understood in relation to God's purpose of grace, Paul is prepared to ascribe to it a positive value.[2] 'The law has been our pedagogue until Christ came, that we might be justified by faith.'[3] But when the law is isolated and exalted into an independent system of religion, it becomes demonic. This corruption of the law is the work of sin, and in particular the sin of self-righteousness. Paul remarks, concerning his fellow Jews, that 'being ignorant of the righteousness which comes from God, and seeking to establish a righteousness of their own, they did not submit to God's righteousness'.[4] All legalism is self-assertion, a claim that we can establish our own righteousness, that we can save ourselves by our own moral and spiritual attainments; and such a claim makes it impossible for us to know God in his true nature as the God of grace.

It is remarkable how, in one passage after another in Paul's epistles, the law duplicates those functions which we have seen elsewhere attributed to Satan. The law is the great accuser: 'all who have sinned under the law

[1] Gal. iii. 19; Rom. v. 20.

[2] Paul uses νόμος in four slightly different senses which must be distinguished, though he himself passes freely from one to another; (1) the O.T. revelation of God, valid but incomplete; (2) the eternal will of God of which the O.T. is a concrete expression; (3) Jewish legalism, which is a misunderstanding of the O.T. revelation; and (4) a similar reign of law among the Gentiles. [3] Gal. iii. 24. [4] Rom. x. 3.

will be judged by the law'; 'we know that whatever the law says it speaks to those who are under the law, that every mouth may be stopped, and the whole world be brought to account before God.'[1]

The law also carries out the sentence. It is the written code which kills, 'the dispensation of death, carved in letters of stone'.[2] It imparts to sin strength and vitality, and the two of them together make death the fearful reality that it has always been in human experience: 'the sting of death is sin and the power of sin is the law';[3] 'I was alive once apart from the law, but when the commandment came, sin revived and I died'. In this last passage Paul is careful to point out that the law in itself is good, and that it becomes a death-dealing force only when mishandled by sin. 'Sin, using the commandment as a base of operations, deceived me and by it killed me.' But a little later we find him dropping his caution and speaking of 'the law of sin and death'.[4]

But besides being prosecutor and executioner the law is also the tempter. 'I should not have had experience of sin except through the law; for I should not have had personal knowledge of covetousness, if the law had not said, Thou shalt not covet. But sin, using the commandment as a base of operations, produced in me all kinds of covetousness.'[5] Paul goes on to say that 'apart from the law sin lies dead'. Evil in itself has no power, no real

---

[1] Rom. ii. 12; iii. 19.　　　　　　　　[2] 2 Cor. iii. 6 f.
[3] 1 Cor. xv. 56.　　　　　　　　[4] Rom. vii. 9 ff.; viii. 2.
[5] Rom. vii. 7 f.　The verbs ἔγνων and ᾔδειν are here commonly mis-translated. Paul uses them in the Hebraic sense of personal knowledge or experience. Cf. 2 Cor. v. 21, where τὸν μὴ γνόντα ἁμαρτίαν means 'him who had no personal acquaintance with sin' (not 'him who knew not the meaning of sin').

existence. It is a parasite, which can exist and thrive and propagate itself only by distorting the good gifts of God. All power belongs to God, and sin can exercise power only by corrupting that which carries the power and authority of God. That is why Paul can say that 'the sting of death is sin and the power of sin is the law'.[1] Through the distortion of sin the law, which embodies a divine authority, becomes a destructive power, actually stimulating men to commit the deeds which its commandments forbid. To escape from sin, therefore, is to escape from the law. 'Sin will have no more dominion over you, since you are not under the law but under grace.'[2]

IV

We must now ask what relationship Paul envisaged between the law as a demonic agency and the principalities and powers. That some such relationship existed in Paul's mind is clear from a passage in Colossians. 'God has made you alive together with Christ, having forgiven all our trespasses, having cancelled the bond which was outstanding against us with its legal demands. And he (sc. Christ) has taken it out of the midst, nailing it to the Cross. He has disarmed the principalities and authorities and exposed them openly, triumphing over them in it [sc. the Cross].'[3] It is the cancelling of the legal bond, the acquittal of men whom the law declares to be sinful and deserving of death, that renders the principalities impotent.

Now there are two possible ways of relating the law to

[1] I Cor. xv. 56.　　　[2] Rom. vi. 14.　　　[3] Col. ii. 13–14.

the powers. Either Paul regarded the law itself as one of the powers, or behind the law he perceived the existence of angelic beings who were responsible for the law's enforcement. There is much to be said in favour of both theories, each of which has had its advocates among the scholars of the past; and there is, of course, no reason why Paul should not have held both points of view at different times or even concurrently.

In Romans the law, sin, and death are personified as a trio of evil forces by which human life is held in bondage: 'death reigned from Adam to Moses . . . sin reigned in death . . . death no longer has dominion over him . . . sin will have no dominion over you, since you are not under the law . . . the law of the spirit of life in Christ Jesus has set me free from the law of sin and death.'[1] It would be quite natural to think that these three are to be reckoned among the principalities and powers of which Paul speaks a little later in the same epistle: 'I am persuaded that neither death, nor life, nor angels, nor principalities, nor things present, nor things to come, nor powers, nor height, nor depth, nor any other created thing, shall be able to separate us from the love of God, which is in Christ Jesus our Lord.'[2] There is another passage, too, where death seems to be ranked among the powers. 'Then comes the end, when he delivers the kingdom to God the Father, when he shall have subdued every principality and every authority and power. For he must reign until he has put all his enemies under his feet. The last enemy to be subdued is death.'[3]

---

[1] Rom. v. 14, 21; vi. 9, 14; viii. 2.
[2] Rom. viii. 38–39.
[3] 1 Cor. xv. 24–26.

Paul is careful to point out, however, that the three tyrants, though they operate as a single destructive team, are not to be identified. 'What then shall we say? That the law is sin? Certainly not!'[1] Sin is intrinsically evil, and therefore intrinsically impotent. It becomes potent only through its alliance with the law. The law is intrinsically good; it carries divine authority, and its purpose is to make men obedient to God's will. It becomes an evil power because sin uses it as a base of operations. The law, therefore, since it is of divine origin, can be regarded as one of the powers in a sense which does not apply to sin, and which does not apply in quite the same way even to death.

In the last chapter we saw that even in its demonic character the state could still fulfil its God-given task of preserving law and order. It is now possible to see that even in its demonic character the law still fulfils a function in the divine economy of salvation. From one point of view the tyranny of the law is the work of sin. But from another point of view it is the work of God, who gave men up in the lusts of their hearts to impurity.[2] It is not the will of God that men should sin, but it is his will, his consequent will, that if they sin they should suffer the consequences. If we stop at this point, however, we leave the world under the control of the principalities and powers. We must add that God can permit the tyranny of law because he knows that beyond law there is grace. 'Law came in to increase the trespass; but where sin increased, grace abounded all the more.'[3] 'God has shut up all men into disobedience, that he may have mercy upon all.'[4]

[1] Rom. vii. 7.   [2] Rom. i. 24.   [3] Rom. v. 20.   [4] Rom. xi. 32.

This point has been admirably expounded by Nygren in his commentary on Romans. 'Like the wrath of God, the law represents God's "strange work", which he must carry out, that he may later effect his "proper work", the work of which the gospel is the message. The law is the means by which sin brings man to death. God can permit sin to use the law in this way, he can permit it to kill man, because in his "proper work", in justification, he gives life to the dead.'[1]

The personification of the law is sufficient to explain Paul's teaching in Romans, but it is inadequate to explain his thought in Colossians or in Galatians. For in Colossians Paul emphatically asserts that the powers are created beings, created in and for Christ, and destined through Christ to be reconciled to God. Sin and death cannot be considered to be among these powers, for they are not created beings nor can they be reconciled to God. The law is a divine creation, but could Paul have said that it was to be reconciled to God? It is true that we can speak metaphorically of reconciling God's justice with his mercy. But properly speaking reconciliation is a transaction between persons. I am not quite sure what is the metaphysical status of a personification, but I seriously doubt whether it could be a party to a reconciliation. We must also take into account the purpose for which Paul wrote the epistle to the Colossians. Against the Colossian heresy, which certainly included the worship of angelic powers, Paul asserts that the independent influence of all such powers has been broken by the Cross, so that they can now be reconciled to God, and restored

[1] A. Nygren, *The Epistle to the Romans*, pp. 281 ff.

to their proper place in the created order under the lordship of Christ. The powers of Colossians, then, who are said to have been defeated in the Cross by the cancelling of the legal charge against men, must be regarded as angelic beings, including the angelic mediators and guardians of the law.

In Galatians Paul refers to a Jewish tradition that the law was given through angels.[1] The origins of this belief are obscure, but the tradition is well attested. It is mentioned in the book of Jubilees, in the Antiquities of Josephus, in the speech of Stephen, and in the Epistle to the Hebrews.[2] Hard upon the mention of this tradition in Galatians there follows a passage of extreme intricacy.[3] Paul points out that in secular law a boy is not allowed control of an inherited estate until a date fixed in his father's will; during his minority he has as little independence as a slave, because he is kept under the discipline of guardians and trustees. He goes on:

Similarly also we [and here he speaks as a Jew addressing churches which were partly Jewish and partly Gentile] during our spiritual minority were enslaved to the elemental spirits of the world. But when the fulness of time came, God sent forth his Son, born of woman, born under law, that he might redeem those who were under law, that we might receive adoption.

The context makes it quite clear that the phrase 'those who were under law' does not refer to Jews only: Jesus did not come to offer redemption and sonship only to

[1] Gal. iii. 19; see also B. Reicke, 'The Law and this World according to Paul', *Journal of Biblical Literature*, lxx (1951), pp. 259–76.
[2] Jub. i. 27; Jos. *Ant.* xv. 5. 3. Acts vii. 53; Heb. ii. 2.
[3] Gal. iv. 1–11.

those who had lived under the Torah. Paul is saying that Jews and Gentiles alike have lived under law, and that for both alike this meant enslavement to the elemental spirits. But Paul now proceeds to say that the Gentiles had formerly been enslaved to those who by nature were not gods. In the case of the Gentiles the elemental spirits are to be identified with those beings whom the Gentile world erroneously regarded as divine. But these Gentiles of Galatia have been converted from paganism to Christianity, and now wish to adopt in addition certain practices of the Jewish law. Paul warns them that to do so would be to 'revert to the weak and beggarly elements, to which you want to be enslaved all over again'. To come in any way under the Torah is to submit to the bondage of those very powers from which Christianity had set them free.

This passage raises two questions of the greatest importance for our understanding of Pauline theology. In the first place, if the elemental spirits are, in the case of the Gentiles, to be identified with the pagan deities, what does Paul mean by saying that the Jews lived under a similar bondage, and that the adoption of Jewish practices constitutes a lapse into the power of the elemental spirits? In the second place, what does Paul mean by saying that the Gentiles lived 'under law'? Does he imply that paganism provided for them a legal discipline and a *praeparatio evangelica* equivalent to that provided for the Jews by the Torah?

We have already seen that in Jewish belief the pagan gods were in reality angelic beings to whom God had delegated some measure of his own authority, but whose

character had become corrupted by an idolatrous worship, which exalted them to a divine and absolute status.
We can now see that to the critical insight of Paul the
angelic mediators of the Torah occupied an analogous
position. They had been made guardians of a revelation
which was both temporary and partial, but which Jewish
orthodoxy had elevated to absolute validity. Thus the
Jew as well as the Gentile was living under an angelic
régime, which rested ultimately on divine institution, but
in which the eternal purpose of God was both distorted
and frustrated.

This régime, for Gentile as well as for Jew, was a
régime of law. There can be little doubt that Paul held
a highly developed doctrine of natural law, which he
derived partly from Jewish and partly from Stoic sources.[1]
He argues that the Gentiles have the capacity to know
God, though few in fact have chosen to exercise it.[2] He is
prepared to admit that among the Gentiles there are men
living, by the light of conscience, lives which compare
favourably with the lives of most Jews.[3] He will attempt
to clinch an argument by appealing to what Nature
herself teaches.[4] And he declares that the legal institutions
of the pagan state rest upon a divine decree.[5] Paul uses
the word νόμος sometimes as the equivalent of Torah,
sometimes in its wider hellenistic sense, so that the concept of revealed law could readily pass over into the
complementary concept of natural law.

[1] See also C. H. Dodd, *New Testament Studies*, pp. 129–42. It is true
that Paul sometimes describes the Gentiles as ἄνομοι (1 Cor. ix. 21 ; cf.
Rom. ii. 12–14), but this means simply that they did not have the Torah.
[2] Rom. i. 19–21.   [3] Rom. ii. 14 f.
[4] 1 Cor. xi. 14.   [5] Rom. xiii. 1.

Five centuries before Paul came to Athens Aeschylus in the *Prometheus Vinctus* and the *Oresteia* had made Greece aware of the conflict between divine goodness and divine justice. But in more recent times Greek thought had come to accept the reign of law as a true interpretation of the divine. Socrates had claimed to be under the control of a δαιμόνιον, which was constantly exercising the right of veto on his proposed actions.[1] The Stoics had taken up this idea of the inner demon, and had made it into a general description of the working of conscience. The word συνείδησις, a technical term of Stoic ethics, was rapidly adopted into popular speech, so that we find Menander, a contemporary of Zeno, saying that 'for all mortals conscience is god'.[2] The great exponent of popular philosophy, Posidonius, declared that the cardinal sin is 'not to follow at all points the inner demon, which has an affinity and a common nature with the power that orders the whole universe'.[3] Similarly Marcus Aurelius can say of his conscience, 'It is impossible for me to do anything contrary to my god and demon'.[4] This Stoic belief in a natural law which made its impact on human life through conscience received a great impetus from the wide dissemination of astrological beliefs. In astrology the heavenly bodies were regarded as divine beings and known as τὰ στοιχεῖα; under the influence of their regular motions the whole of human life was controlled by bonds of inexorable necessity. Thus when the Greeks identified the five planets with the five major gods of their pantheon

---

[1] Plato, *Apol.* 31 c–d; cf. Xen. *Mem.* 1. 2.
[2] *Monostichoi,* 671 : βροτοῖς ἅπασιν ἡ συνείδησις θεός.
[3] Galen, *De Hipp. et Plat.* 5. 6.
[4] v. 10; cf. ii. 13, v. 27; Epict. *Diss.* i. 14, ii. 22.

a great change overtook Greek religion. The Olympic gods had been capricious and unpredictable in their behaviour, but the motions of the planets were reliable, law abiding, calculable. With the advent of astrology the anthropomorphic gods had begun to give place to 'the army of unalterable law'. The iron rule of an impersonal fate robbed life both of meaning and of hope, and no small part of the appeal of Paul's preaching must have been that it offered release from servitude to the elemental spirits.[1] Yet at the same time astrology with its reign of law gave to the polytheistic world a valuable preparation for the coming of a monotheistic religion.

V

The demonic forces of legalism, then, both Jewish and Gentile, can be called 'principalities and powers' or 'elemental spirits of the world'. In another epistle we find a similar link between the law and 'the god of this age'.[2] In the course of a detailed contrast between the partial and transient glory of the old covenant and the perfect and abiding glory of the new covenant, Paul refers to the passage in Exodus in which it is said that Moses, on descending from Mount Sinai, had to cover his face with a veil, because it shone with a reflection of God's glory which the Israelites could not bear to look upon. His comment is that 'to this day at the reading of the old covenant the same veil remains unlifted, because only in Christ is it removed. To this day whenever Moses is read

[1] For the longing of the ancient world for freedom from the dominion of the stars see Apuleius, *Met.* xi. 6.
[2] 2 Cor. iv. 4.

a veil lies upon their hearts.'[1] The law, which should have revealed God to his people, has in fact hidden him from them, and has hidden him so effectively that they were unable to recognize the greater manifestation of his glory in Jesus Christ. Paul is careful, however, not to leave the impression that the law, in itself, is hostile to the purposes of God. It is the god of this age who has used the law as a means of blinding 'the minds of unbelievers to prevent them from seeing the light of the gospel of the glory of Christ, who is the image of God'.[2]

In the first chapter I suggested that the development of Paul's thinking about principalities and powers owed something to his experience of Roman imperial administration. I would now suggest that his belief in the existence of demonic powers behind the law owed a very great deal to his own religious experience. For Paul had been an enthusiastic devotee of the Torah, determined to establish his own righteousness by obedience to its commands. He had been a Pharisee; indeed, the standards of Pharisaism had not satisfied him; he must surpass the attainments of his contemporaries.[3] His zeal for the law had led him to repudiate Jesus as a blasphemer who had died under the curse of the law.[4] It had led him to persecute the church, whose existence seemed to him to be an affront to God's honour.[5] Then in a flash of illumination he had seen the glory of God in the face of Jesus Christ, and in the light of that experience he saw his past life exposed in all its contradiction. He who had thought to possess in the law the complete and final revelation of

---

[1] 2 Cor. iii. 14 f.   [2] 2 Cor. iv. 4.   [3] Phil. iii. 5–6; Gal. i. 14.
[4] Gal. iii. 13.   [5] Gal. i. 13; Phil. iii. 6

God had failed to recognize God in the person of his Son. In defending the honour of God's law he had become the enemy of God. And what was true of Paul was true of the Jews in general. It was not their irreligion but their religion, their enthusiasm for the Torah, which had crucified the Son of God. The law had lain like a veil across their hearts to prevent them from seeing that God had visited and redeemed his people.

But how did the law, holy, just, and good as it was, produce such terrifying results? Paul's treatment of the law bears at every point the indelible mark of that moment in his own spiritual history when he had realized that everything he had regarded as highest and best had combined to put Christ on the Cross. His doctrine of principalities and powers provided him with an answer to this intensely personal problem. All power and authority belongs to God, and evil can exist as a force in the world only because it is able to take the powers and authorities of God and to transform them into world-rulers of this darkness. So it had come about that Israel and Rome, the highest religion and the best government that the world had seen, had conspired to crucify the Lord of Glory.

III

The Bondage of Corruption

I

THE Old Testament attitude to nature rests upon two fundamental beliefs: that God is Lord of nature; and that God uses nature to further a moral purpose which has its centre in man. In this chapter we shall be concerned chiefly with the exceptions to these two rules, but I propose at the outset to enlarge upon the rules themselves in order that we may better appreciate the significance of the exceptions.

W. Robertson Smith has shown that, in the primitive stages of Semitic religion, the belief in a divine control of nature grew in proportion to man's ability to subdue his natural environment.

In fact the earth may be said to be parcelled out between demons and wild beasts on the one hand, and gods and men on the other. To the former belong the untrodden wilderness with all its unknown perils, the wastes and jungles that lie outside the familiar tracks and pasture grounds of the tribe, and which only the boldest men venture upon without terror; to the latter belong the regions that man knows and habitually frequents, and within which he has established relations, not only with his human neighbours, but with the supernatural beings that have their haunts side by side with him. And as man gradually encroaches on the wilderness and drives back the wild beasts before him, so the gods in like manner drive out the demons, and spots that were once feared, as the habitation of mysterious and presumably malignant powers, lose their terrors and either become common ground or are transformed into the seats of friendly deities. From this point of view the recognition of certain spots as haunts of the gods is the religious expression of the gradual subjugation of nature by man.[1]

It is a far cry from this type of religion to Paul's belief in the cosmic Christ, but I hope to be able to show that the one is the lineal descendant of the other. For already in this primitive religion we can see the beginnings of the idea that God's supremacy over the universe is inseparably bound up with the lordship of man.

The growth of religion in Israel cannot be understood apart from this background of common Semitic religion; nor can it be understood simply as evolution, as the result of natural causes. It was because of the special revelation which she had received in history, interpreted by the prophets from Moses to Deutero-Isaiah, that Israel was able to rise above the general religious level to attain to her monotheistic faith. The primary tenet of this revealed faith was that God was Lord of history. He had brought Israel up out of the land of Egypt, from the house of bondage, and could be expected to perform similar acts of deliverance in the hour of his people's need. But in his historic act of salvation God had shown that certain forces of nature were at the disposal of his sovereign will.

Thou didst blow with thy wind, the sea covered them:
They sank as lead in the mighty waters.[2]

[1] *The Religion of the Semites*, 3rd ed., pp. 121 f.
[2] Exod. xv. 10.

When the waters saw thee, O God,
When the waters saw thee, they were afraid;
Yea, the depths trembled.
The clouds poured out water;
The skies uttered their voice;
Yea, thine arrows flashed all around.
The voice of thy thunder was in the whirlwind;
The lightnings lit up the world;
The earth trembled and shook.
Thy way was through the sea,
Thy path through the great waters,
Yet thy footsteps were not seen.
Thou didst lead thy people like a flock
By the hand of Moses and Aaron.[1]

As the religion of Israel developed, therefore, the sphere
of Yahweh's sovereignty was steadily extended until it
became commensurate with the universe.

In the first chapter I alluded to the process whereby
the Canaanite nature deities either surrendered their
attributes to Yahweh or took subordinate office under
his supreme command as ministering angels. Along with
this development came a growing realization of the
stability of the natural order. God had established the
heavenly bodies to mark out regular seasons.[2] The animal
creation, too, obeyed an unchanging divine decree.

Even the stork in the heavens knows her times;
And the turtledove, swallow, and crane keep the time of their
      coming;
But my people know not the ordinance of the Lord.[3]

But Israel never had a conception of natural law operat-
ing independently of the personal agency of God. Indeed,

---

[1] Ps. lxxvii. 16–20.   [2] Gen. i. 14; Ps. civ. 19.   [3] Jer. viii. 7.

the Old Testament knows of no distinction between natural and miraculous events: all events are equally supernatural. The one word *niphla'oth* ('wondrous works' or 'marvels') is used frequently to describe any works of God in creation or providence which have excited the abiding admiration of his worshipping people. Nature, then, is stable: but its stability depends upon the trustworthiness of God: 'all his work is done in faithfulness.'[1] Nature is dependable because God remains true to himself and true to his promises: 'While earth remains, seedtime and harvest, cold and heat, summer and winter, day and night shall not cease.'[2]

But this process, whereby all nature was reduced to an orderly system under the providential government of God, was never quite completed. There were always some recalcitrant elements which refused to be brought within the scope of the divine sovereignty. Some of the less reputable objects of Canaanite worship could not be naturalized within the religion of Yahweh, and, although theoretically suppressed, they were in fact relegated to a kind of nightmare fringe of popular superstition. Saul is credited with having put down necromancy, only to break his own prohibition by consulting the witch of Endor;[3] and four centuries later the Deuteronomic legislators still found it necessary to include in their code a law forbidding, among other forms of divination, the consulting of ghosts and familiar spirits.[4] Besides these there were the *Shedim*, to whom an idolatrous worship was offered;[5] *Azazel*, for whom a goat was dispatched annually

---

[1] Ps. xxxiii. 4.   [2] Gen. viii. 22.   [3] 1 Sam. xxviii. 3 ff.
[4] Deut. xviii. 10 f.   [5] Deut. xxxii. 17; Ps. cvi. 37.

into the wilderness in a ritual which was hallowed by its incorporation into the Levitical code;[1] and the *Se'irim* (satyrs) and *Lilith* (the night hag), who together with uncanny beasts were believed to inhabit the ruins of dead cities. These denizens of desolation are mentioned in two passages in the book of Isaiah, which give a vivid picture of the doom in store for Babylon and Edom.

> It shall be uninhabited for ever
> Nor shall it be dwelt in to all generations;
> The Arab shall not pitch tent there,
> Nor shall shepherds make their flocks to lie down there.
> But wild-cats shall make their dens there,
> And their houses shall be full of howlers.
> There shall ostriches dwell,
> And satyrs shall dance there.
> Hyenas shall cry in their mansions,
> And jackals in their pleasant palaces.[2]
>
> Thorns shall come up in her palaces,
> Nettles and thistles in her fortresses.
> It shall be a habitation for jackals,
> A court for ostriches.
> The wild-cats shall meet with the hyenas,
> And the satyr shall cry to his fellow;
> Yea, the night hag shall settle there
> And find for herself a resting place.
> There the owl shall make her nest
> And lay and hatch and gather under her shadow;
> Yea, there shall the kites be gathered,
> Every one with her mate.[3]

I have quoted these passages at length because they describe a consorting of animals with demons which can-

[1] Lev. xvi. 7 ff.   [2] Isa. xiii. 20–22.   [3] Isa. xxxiv. 13–15.

not be dismissed as mere superstition.[1] They testify to the existence of a strong popular feeling that not only in human life but in the world of nature there is a residue which cannot be brought into congruity with the holiness of God. Further evidence for this is to be found in the distinction between the clean and the unclean beasts. Among creatures which the Levitical code declares to be unclean, and therefore unfit for human consumption, are all beasts and birds of prey. Now the laws of uncleanness may very well be survivals of primitive taboo, and the uncleanness of beasts and birds of prey may very well be due to the fact that they violate one of the most primitive taboos by eating the blood of their victims. But when every allowance has been made for what the anthropologists have to tell us about the irrational nature of taboo, are we not dealing here with a naïve expression of the idea that nature red in tooth and claw has in some measure escaped the control of the divine holiness?

It may be objected that to contrast the holy with the

---

[1] The identification of some of the creatures mentioned in these two passages is highly conjectural. Some commentators have felt, however, that if we could identify them all beyond doubt, the lists would prove to contain only wild beasts, without any suggestion of demons. Thus they would translate *se'irim* not as 'satyrs' but as 'he-goats'. To this interpretation there are three objections: (1) when *sa'ir* means 'he-goat' it always refers to the domestic goat, not to the wild goat, which is either *ya'el* or *'aqqo*; (2) there are two passages in which *se'irim* refers undoubtedly to the objects of idolatrous worship, i.e. goat gods (Lev. xvii. 7; 2 Chr. xi. 15); (3) the LXX translation in each of the passages from Isaiah is δαιμόνια, and this rendering is more likely to be the product of traditional interpretation than of the admittedly erratic methods of the translator of Isaiah. For these reasons I prefer the more generally accepted rendering 'satyrs'. But in any case it is dubious whether popular belief in ancient times would have drawn any distinction between demons in animal form and animals with demonic associations. On the demonic character of the ostrich, see W. R. Smith, op. cit., p. 129.

unclean is to confuse two categories of thought, since the opposite of holy is common and the opposite of unclean is clean. But in fact the two sets of terms belong together, and common and clean are but colourless negations of their opposites. The holy is that which is withdrawn from the normal life of men through dedication to a deity; and all else is common. The unclean is that which is withdrawn from the normal life of men because of an inherent disqualification; and all else is clean. Both conceptions are derived from taboo.

A common thing may become taboo if a god or a sacred person lays a taboo upon it. Or a thing or state may be intrinsically taboo. Roughly speaking, this corresponds to the distinction between holy and unclean. The holy is that which is naturally common, but has become holy through contact with the Divine. But there is an uncleanness of a primary order, of an intrinsic and not accidental kind, uncommunicated as no earthly holiness can be said to be.[1]

In other words, all objects and persons belong to one of three classes: that which is both clean and common, and to which therefore no disability attaches; that which is clean but holy; and that which is common but unclean. The unclean is that which is inherently unfit for human use; but, since all that is fit for human use is fit also to be offered to God, the unclean is that which cannot in any circumstances become holy.

Quite a different illustration of the incompleteness of God's sovereignty over nature is provided by the recurrent use of the Creation myth. In the Babylonian myth, from which the Genesis story was adapted, either directly

[1] A. S. Peake, *Hastings' Dictionary of the Bible*, iv, p. 826.

or through Canaanite sources, the god Marduk cut in two the primeval ocean dragon, and of the two halves of her body made earth and heaven. The dragon was called either Apsu or Tiamat, but appears in the Old Testament under the names Rahab, Leviathan, and Tehom Rabbah (the Great Deep). In the theology of the Old Testament this myth came to be combined with the Exodus tradition. Just as God at the Creation had cleft in two the waters of ocean to create an ordered universe, so at the Exodus he had cleft in two the waters of the Red Sea to provide a passage for his ransomed people. In terms derived from the Creation myth the psalmist describes Israel's salvation:

Thou didst divide the sea by thy strength:
Thou didst break the heads of the dragon in the waters.
Thou didst break the heads of Leviathan,
That thou mightest give them for food to the folk of the jackals.[1]

Similarly, Deutero-Isaiah cites the double victory of God over the dragon at the Creation and at the Exodus as the basis of a hope for a new Exodus:

Awake, awake, put on strength, O arm of the Lord;
Awake, as in days of old, the generations of ancient times.
Art thou not he who cut Rahab in pieces, who pierced the
    dragon?
Art thou not he who dried up the sea, the waters of the Great
    Deep?
That made the depths of the sea a way for the redeemed to
    pass over?[2]

---

[1] Ps. lxxiv. 13–14. This use of mythological language to describe the Exodus may help to account for the change which took place between the J story, in which the crossing of the sea was made possible by a strong east wind, and the P story, in which the sea was divided so as to stand in two solid walls.

[2] Isa. li. 9–10. See also H. G. May, 'Some Cosmic Connotations of Mayim Rabbim', *Journal of Biblical Literature*, lxxiv (1955), pp. 9–22.

Thus it became a part of the eschatological expectation of Israel that God would achieve a final triumph over the ocean dragon—that reservoir of all evil. 'In that day the Lord with his hard and great and strong sword shall punish Leviathan the fleeing serpent, and Leviathan the crooked serpent, and shall slay the dragon that is in the sea.'[1] This use of the Creation myth to depict God's victory over evil implies that the problem of evil presented itself as a cosmic problem.

It is worth while to notice in passing that the Creation myth plays a large part in the symbolism of Revelation. The crystal sea in heaven represents all that bars man from access to the throne of God.[2] Out of the sea rises the beast, which is both the parody and the usurper of God's authority.[3] Like the Red Sea before the Israelites, the heavenly sea parts to allow the martyr throng to pass into the security of the promised land, and having passed they sing the song of Moses and the Lamb.[4] As the Red Sea returned to its strength to overwhelm the Egyptians, so the heavenly sea is poured from the seven vials of wrath to engulf the enemies of God.[5] And when the victory of God is complete the heavenly city is revealed, in which there is no more sea.[6]

There was one point where Israel's doubts about the sovereignty of God came to a sharp focus—Sheol. The Old Testament has a remarkable and descriptive list of synonyms for Sheol: it is the grave, the pit, corruption, Abaddon (the destroyer), the dust, death, darkness, silence, oblivion; it is the house appointed for all the

---

[1] Isa. xxvii. 1.   [2] Rev. iv. 6.   [3] Rev. xiii. 1.
[4] Rev. xv.   [5] Rev. xvi.   [6] Rev. xxi. 1.

living. The common assumption which underlies most of the descriptions of Sheol is that it lies outside God's dominion.

> Wilt thou show thy wonders to the dead?
> Shall the shades arise and praise thee?
> Shall thy lovingkindness be declared in the grave?
> Or thy faithfulness in Abaddon?
> Shall thy wonders be known in the dark?
> And thy righteousness in the land of oblivion?[1]

Occasionally men are warned that even Sheol provides no escape from the pursuing 'hound of heaven'.[2] But these passages do little to mitigate the general impression that the very existence of Sheol is an affront to him who is the God of the living. This impression is strongly reinforced by the priestly code in which it is laid down that any contact with death causes uncleanness of a particularly virulent kind.[3] Even the development of a doctrine of resurrection did not seriously alter the conception of Sheol, which remained an enemy to be overcome in God's final act of salvation.

II

Let us now turn to the second of the basic Old Testament beliefs about nature. H. W. Robinson has said that 'the Old Testament regards Nature, in the last resort, simply as the arena for the moral issues of human life'.[4] Man differs from the rest of creation in that he is made in the image of God, made for fellowship with God. The one

---

[1] Ps. lxxxviii. 10–12; cf. vi. 5; xxx. 9; Isa. xxxviii. 18.
[2] Ps. cxxxix. 7–8; cf. Prov. xv. 1; Job xxvi. 6; Am. ix. 2.
[3] Num. xix. 11 ff.
[4] *Religious Ideas of the Old Testament*, p. 72.

condition of such fellowship is willing obedience, and to
the moral discipline of man all creation is made to con-
tribute. In one of the prophecies of Hosea, for example,
the orderly processes of nature provide a chain of
messengers to convey to man the gospel of God's for-
giveness.

In that day, says the Lord,
I will answer the heavens and they shall answer the earth;
And the earth shall answer the grain, the wine, and the oil;
And they shall answer Jezreel.[1]

On the other hand natural disorders may convey to man
God's warning and chastisement.

I have smitten you with blasting and mildew:
The multitude of your gardens and your vineyards
And your fig trees and your olive trees has the palmerworm
    devoured;
Yet have you not returned to me, says the Lord.[2]

I will restore to you the years
Which the swarming locust has eaten,
The cankerworm and the caterpillar and the palmerworm,
My great army which I sent among you.[3]

Frequently the works of God are put forward as an elo-
quent summons to men to praise the Lord for his goodness,[4] and sometimes they are offered as an object lesson
in obedience.

The ox knows its owner
And the ass its master's crib,
But Israel does not know,
My people do not understand.[5]

---

[1] Hos. ii. 21 f.   [2] Am. iv. 9.   [3] Joel ii. 25.
[4] e.g. Ps. cvii.   [5] Isa. i. 3.

We may freely admit that such passages as these represent the normal attitude of the Old Testament towards nature. Yet here and there we find passages which remind us that nature is not fully explained by its subservience to the education of man, that God is interested in creation for its own sake, and that the subhuman creation is too intimately related to man to be a mere backcloth to his spiritual drama. The book of Job, for example, ends with a magnificent protest against any narrowly anthropocentric and utilitarian conception of the universe. The ox may know its owner and the ass its master's crib, but what of the wild ass which scorns the shouts of the driver and the wild ox which has never bowed its neck to the yoke? What of the ostrich, the eagle, the crocodile, the hippopotamus? Elsewhere we find reminders that the things which distinguish man from the lower creation are not the whole truth about him. On the physical side he is a child of nature. Like all other creatures he has been taken out of the dust and to dust he must return.[1] While God is spirit, man, like the beasts, is flesh, and the flesh constitutes a bond of union with the whole animal kingdom.[2] The phrase 'all flesh' commonly designates all mankind, but it may be used to include 'every living creature in whose nostrils is the breath of life'.[3] Man's flesh is the mark of his frailty and mortality, and indicates that he belongs among the beasts that perish.[4]

The solidarity of man with the rest of creation is so close that in some way or other nature must bear the conse-

[1] Gen. ii. 7, 19; cf. Ps. ciii. 14 ff.; Eccl. xii. 7.   [2] Isa. xxxi. 3.
[3] Gen. vii. 21; cf. Gen. vi. 17, 19; vii. 15, 16; viii. 17; ix. 11, 15, 16, 17; Lev. xvii. 11, 14; Num. xviii. 15; Ps. cxxxvi. 25.
[4] Ps. xlix. 12, 20.

quences of men's sin. God declares to Adam: 'Cursed be
the ground for your sake; in sorrow shall you eat of it all
the days of your life; thorns also and thistles shall it bring
forth to you.'[1] Jeremiah carries the same idea to greater
lengths by predicting the return of chaos as part of the
retribution which must overtake the sins of men.

> I looked at the earth, and lo, it was waste and void;
> And to the heavens, and they had no light.
> I looked at the mountains, and lo, they were quaking;
> And all the hills moved to and fro.
> I looked, and lo, there was no man;
> And all the birds of the air had fled.
> I looked, and lo, the fruitful land was a desert;
> And all its cities lay in ruins
> Before the Lord and before his fierce anger.[2]

The reverse of this process can be seen in those beautiful
passages in which, with the reconciliation of man to God,
nature regains the splendour of the Garden of Eden.

The wolf shall dwell with the lamb,
And the leopard shall lie down with the kid,
And the calf and the young lion and the fatling together,
And a little child shall lead them.
The cow and the bear shall feed;
Their young shall lie down together;
And the lion shall eat straw like the ox.
The sucking child shall play on the hole of the asp,
And the weaned child shall put his hand on the adder's den.
They shall not hurt nor destroy in all my holy mountain;
For the earth shall be full of the knowledge of the Lord
As the waters cover the sea.[3]

----

[1] Gen. iii. 17 f.   [2] Jer. iv. 23–26.   [3] Isa. xi. 6–9.

Most of these passages are found in the book of Isaiah,[1] so that it is interesting to find a similar idea in an entirely different source—the book of Job, where the promise that man may be at peace with nature is not deferred to the eschatological future.

> At destruction and famine you shall laugh,
> And shall not fear the beasts of the earth.
> For you shall have a covenant with the stones of the field,
> And the beasts of the field shall be at peace with you.[2]

This theme was further elaborated in the later Jewish literature. The book of Jubilee declares that through man's sin the animals lost the power of speech and were driven out of Eden.[3] Bereshith Rabbah tells us that through Adam the courses of the planets were changed, the earth and heavenly bodies lost their former brightness, and death came upon all living creatures.[4] And the Apocalypse of Baruch broods deeply upon the mystery of corruption: 'How long will that which is corruptible remain? . . . Bring to an end therefore henceforth mortality and reprove the angel of death.'[5] A popular legend also grew up around the story of the sons of God who lusted after the daughters of men.[6] It was held that from this union had sprung a race of evil spirits, who were responsible for introducing all manner of evils into the world, and in particular had seduced men into an idolatrous worship.[7] It must not be thought, however, that this theory in any way transferred the guilt of sin from man to the fallen angels. The fall of the angels—the

[1] Isa. xxxv. 1–2; lv. 12–13; lxv. 17–25; lxvi. 22.
[2] Job v. 22 f.   [3] Jub. iii. 28 f.   [4] Bereshith R. 12–19.
[5] 2 Bar. xxi. 19–23.   [6] Gen. vi. 1–4.   [7] En. xix. 1; Bar. iv. 7.

Watchers, as they were called—is not a precosmic event, as in Milton's *Paradise Lost*. In most Jewish literature it was on account of mankind that the angels fell.[1] The Apocalypse of Baruch even goes so far as to say that it was the physical nature of man which not only 'became a danger to his own soul' but resulted in the fall of the angels.[2]

The modern mind, accustomed to theories of evolution, finds it a little hard to lay at man's door all the evils of the subhuman creation. We do not need Scripture to tell us that man's ignorance and greed may turn a paradise into a dust bowl; but this does not seem to provide an all-sufficient explanation of cosmic evil. The Apocalypse of Moses, however, although in general it shares the presuppositions of the other apocalyptic and Rabbinic writings, has a somewhat different approach to the problem, which is capable of adaptation to modern needs, and which is important for our understanding of the New Testament. There we are told that through the sin of Adam the animals ceased to obey man. A wild beast attacks Seth and then explains to Eve: 'It is from thee that the rule of the beasts has arisen.'[3] In modern terms does not this mean that God meant man to exercise dominion over all his creatures, and that only under man's control was the universe to find its meaning and purpose? Without man as master creation is like an arch without its keystone. Through his sin man has repudiated his divinely ordained authority, has vacated his viceregal throne, has become a mere part of the creation of which

---

[1] The chief exception is Slav. En. xxix. 4 ff.
[2] 2 Bar. lvi. 10–13.   [3] Apoc. Mos. 10 f.

he was destined to be lord, and has abandoned the universe to the sway of more sinister powers.

This conception of man's destiny helps us to understand the night vision of Daniel, in which the prophet predicts that the world empires of the past are to give place to the kingdom of the saints of the Most High. Exegesis has usually concentrated on the substance of this prophecy to the neglect of the symbolism in which it is expressed. For the worldly empires are symbolized by four beasts and the kingdom of God by 'one like to a son of man'.[1] We are meant to understand that the coming of the kingdom involves not only the victory of good over evil in human affairs, but also the restoration of man to lordship over the beasts, the reassertion of God's purpose to exalt the son of man, to 'put all things in subjection under his feet, all sheep and oxen, yea, and the beasts of the field'.[2]

III

Many of the ideas we have so far been discussing in their Old Testament setting are taken up by the Synoptists to provide a background to the ministry of Jesus, and it is more than likely that they do so on the authority of Jesus himself. Matthew and Luke record sayings of Jesus which prove that he himself thought of his ministry as a battle against the powers of evil. He taught his disciples to pray that they might be delivered from the Evil One,[3] and warned them that the Enemy was always busy sowing weeds among God's harvest.[4] He told them the story of

---

[1] Dan. vii. 1–13.
[2] Ps. viii. 6 ff.
[3] Mt. vi. 13.
[4] Mt. xiii. 28.

his own temptation, when the Devil had claimed that all worldly authority was his to bestow, and, according to Luke's version, was his by divine permission.[1] The authority of Satan was seen in physical disease,[2] in demon possession,[3] in moral evil or weakness,[4] and above all in the Cross: 'this is your hour and the dominion of darkness.'[5]

But it is in Mark's Gospel that we find the theme most fully developed. The story begins with a proclamation by John the Baptist that a Mightier One is coming after him. With what enemies is the Coming One to do battle? The answer follows immediately when we are told that Jesus went out into the wilderness to be tempted by Satan. This is the preliminary engagement of a campaign which is to last throughout the ministry. Mark adds that 'he was with the wild beasts'[6]—a delicate way of indicating that the problem of evil with which Jesus has come to wrestle is not confined to human affairs. In the story of the ministry which follows, exorcisms bulk large, some of them being the cure of psychological or spiritual disorders, others involving physical cures as well; and it is interesting to notice that Mark frequently refers to the demons as 'unclean spirits', thus reminding us of the connexion which we have found to subsist between the unclean and the demonic. When Jesus is accused of casting out demons

---

[1] Mt. iv. 9; Lk. iv. 6. With ἐμοὶ παραδέδοται cf. Rev. xiii. 5: καὶ ἐδόθη αὐτῷ ἐξουσία.

[2] Lk. xiii. 16. H. Loewe (*Encyclopaedia of Religion and Ethics*, iv, pp. 612 ff.) suggests that one reason for the common attribution of disease to demonic influence was the lack of abstract nouns in Hebrew, and supports his thesis with a wealth of citation; but we must beware of too much rationalization.

[3] Lk. xi. 14–20.

[4] Lk. xxii. 3, 31.   [5] Lk. xxii. 53.   [6] Mk. i. 13.

by the power of Satan, he replies: 'No one can enter the strong man's house and plunder his goods, unless he first bind the strong man; then he may plunder his house.'[1] The cures of Jesus are proof that into a world dominated by Satanic forces there has come one stronger than Satan. According to the Parable of the Sower Satan tries to frustrate the work of the Gospel, but, in spite of small successes, fails to prevent the final triumph of harvest. A little later we hear of the man whose name is Legion; just as Palestine was territory occupied by a Roman legion, so this man is enemy-occupied territory, and upon him Jesus comes like a liberating army to drive out the invader.

But Mark clearly believed that Jesus' power extended not only over the demons but over the world of nature: he stills the tempest, feeds the multitude, walks upon the water, and rides into Jerusalem on an unbroken colt.[2] It

---

[1] Mk. iii. 27.

[2] Matthew and John, whose accounts of the Triumphal Entry are manifestly independent of one another, both affirm that the animal was a donkey, and both take the incident to be a fulfilment of the prophecy of Zech. ix. 9. Indeed, Matthew, misunderstanding the parallelism of Hebrew verse, tries to make the fulfilment more accurate by introducing two donkeys into the story. He also omits Mark's clause 'on which no one has ever sat', since to him the point of the incident was that it fulfilled a prophecy. But to Mark, who does not mention the prophecy, and who even leaves it an open question whether the animal was a donkey or a horse, the signficant fact was that Jesus could control an unbroken mount. Luke, who follows Mark's account closely at this point, seems to have read into it an interpretation of his own. For there is a subtle parallelism between his accounts of the Triumphal Entry and of the Burial. The colt was one 'on which no man had ever sat' (Lk. xix. 30); the grave was one 'in which no man had ever lain' (Lk. xxiii. 53). Both were unsullied by human use. But Mark has no such parallel description of the grave, and we must not make the mistake of reading back into Mark's Gospel an idea which evidently originated with Luke.

is no wonder, then, that this Jesus should raise questions in the minds of men. 'What is this,' says the crowd, 'a new teaching with authority? He commands even the unclean spirits and they obey him.'[1] 'Who then is this,' ask the disciples, 'that even the wind and the waves obey him?'[2] The crowd think he is a prophet, and the disciples believe him to be the Messiah; but in the recorded sayings of Jesus Mark finds a better answer: He is Son of Man. Like the symbolic figure of Daniel's vision, this Son of Man has come not simply as the representative of God's kingdom, but also to reassert man's lordship over a demonic and rebellious creation. The ministry of Jesus is the process by which God makes good his promise to the Son of Man that he will put all things in subjection under his feet. It is along these lines that we must explain the answer of Jesus to the Pharisees who accused him of breaking the Sabbath. The Sabbath, like everything else in God's creation, was made for man. Therefore the Son of Man, who comes to exercise man's God-given lordship, is lord also of the Sabbath.[3]

IV

Such were the ideas which Paul inherited on the Jewish and Christian side. But in his conception of nature more than in anything else Paul was a debtor to the Greeks, and it was from them that he learnt to view nature as 'one stupendous whole', united by a bond of common frailty. The Greek quest for the one that lies behind the many had reached its climax in the Stoic doctrine of

---

[1] Mk. i. 27.   [2] Mk. iv. 41.   [3] Mk. ii. 28.

cosmic sympathy. They taught that, as in the microcosm whatever affects one part of the body affects the body as a whole, so in the macrocosm there is ἡ τοῦ παντὸς ἕνωσίς τε καὶ συμπάθεια—'the unity and sympathy of the whole'— which holds all things together in a single vast organism.[1]

The desire of the Greeks to discover a unity within the manifold facts of experience arose to a large extent out of the realism with which they regarded the phenomena of change and decay, and this disposition of the Greek mind must have had its influence on the apostle to the Gentiles. The popularity of the mystery religions shows us how firmly the Greek world had been gripped by a horror of death and by a yearning for that immortality which the mysteries professed to offer. Greek philosophy had been greatly preoccupied with the problem of penetrating to something permanent behind the world of γένεσις and φθορά, of generation and corruption, of growth and decay. Political events, too, had added to the general mood of depression, as men felt themselves thrust to the very brink of catastrophe by forces they could neither understand nor control. There is an inscription from Priene which says that the world would have suffered speedy dissolution (φθορά) had it not been for the birth of Augustus.[2] In a similar vein Vergil wrote his fourth Eclogue, acclaiming the advent of the Golden Age in which all nature was returning to its primeval perfection,

> glorying
> in the blissful years again to be,
> Summers of the snakeless meadow,
> unlaborious earth and oarless sea.

[1] Von Arnim, *Stoicorum Veterum Fragmenta*, ii, p. 156; cf. pp. 170, 172, 302, 347.   [2] Priene Inscr. 105[2].

No doubt both the Priene inscription and Vergil's Eclogue contain studied flattery, but it is flattery which reveals to us the line along which the thoughts of men were inclined to travel. Above all, astrology, with its rule of inexorable law, had inculcated into men's hearts a sense of all-pervading futility. When Paul declares that the whole creation has been subjected to futility, and later affirms his faith that neither height nor depth can separate the Christian from the love of God, he shows that he was aware of the stultifying influence of astrology upon the Greek spirit.[1]

We may now pause to observe that the theme we are investigating is falling into a familiar pattern. Like the angelic guardians of the pagan state and the angelic guardians of the Torah, the powers of nature are created beings who can still fulfil something of the purpose for which they were created, in spite of having undergone a corruption which has frustrated the full realization of that purpose and has turned them into enemies of God. For the sake of clarity we have analysed the concept of principalities and powers into these three elements, but we must remember that such distinctions were less obvious in antiquity than they are to us. The deities of the pagan state were responsible for the maintenance of law and had been identified with the astrological gods who represented the reign of natural law. Thus it was possible for the mind of Paul to move by free association from one connotation to another. This does not mean that whenever he mentions the powers he has in the fore-

[1] Rom. viii. 20, 39. On the astrological significance of height and depth see H. Lietzmann, Romans, ad loc.

front of his mind the whole complex of ideas which we have been discussing; but it does mean that when he refers to one aspect of the subject other aspects are always present in the background.

V

Whatever Paul may have owed to those who went before him, both Jews and Greeks, he had a thoroughly personal reason for being interested in the problem of physical suffering and death. Throughout his life he was subject to recurrent attacks of an illness to which he refers as his 'thorn in the flesh'.[1] He speaks of it with the same ambiguity which, as we have seen, attaches to all attempts to describe the demonic. It is God's gift to him to keep him humble, but it is also an angel of Satan. This illness was constantly frustrating his work. He tells the Thessalonians that, during his stay at Athens, he wanted again and again to visit them, but Satan hindered him;[2] and there is every reason to believe that Satan employed for this purpose the angel of ill health, for we know that shortly afterwards Paul arrived in Corinth 'in weakness and in much fear and trembling'.[3] The effects of this illness, combined with the rigours of his long journeys and the ill treatment to which he so often fell victim,

---

[1] 2 Cor. xii. 7. It has sometimes been suggested that the thorn in the flesh must have been a person, since σκόλοψ is used in the LXX of human irritants (Num. xxxiii. 55; Ezek. xxviii. 24). But the demonic character of the affliction is against this; and in any case Paul, being unmarried, had no one—no nagging wife or rebellious child—whose life was linked with his own beyond the possibility of separation, no one from whom relief could be sought only in prayer.

[2] 1 Thess. ii. 18.   [3] 1 Cor. ii. 3.

undermined Paul's naturally robust constitution, and gave him first-hand experience of the bondage of decay. He can write to Corinth: 'Even if my outer man is wasting away, yet my inner man is renewed from day to day.'[1]

Surely it was through the intensity of this experience that Paul came to appreciate the universal sympathy of the Stoics, and reached out towards an empathy with the enslaved cosmos beyond anything that even the Stoics had contemplated. For he pictures the cosmos and himself groaning in unison, the one yearning to be freed from futility, the other impatient at the restrictions imposed upon him by his physical body.

The creation is waiting with eager expectation for the revelation of the sons of God. For the creation was made subject to futility, not of its own will, but through him who subjected it in hope; because the creation itself will be set free from the bondage of decay into the liberty of the glory of the children of God. For we know that the whole creation groans and travails together until now; and not only so, but we ourselves also who have the firstfruits of the Spirit, we groan within ourselves as we wait for adoption, the redemption of our body.[2]

Some scholars have wished to simplify Paul's thought at this point by restricting the reference of the word κτίσις to humankind.[3] But Paul has already said earlier in this epistle that it was through men's own will, through their own deliberate and sinful refusal to acknowledge God, that they have become futile in their own thoughts and have

---

[1] 2 Cor. iv. 16.   [2] Rom. viii. 19–23.
[3] e.g. A. Schlatter, *Gottes Gerechtigkeit*, pp. 269 ff.; E. Brunner, *Revelation and Reason*, p. 72.

been abandoned by God to the consequences of their own choice.[1] We cannot therefore suppose that in the present passage he is contradicting himself by saying that the human race has been subjected to futility, not by its own will but by the will of God. Rather he is declaring that the futility of the subhuman creation is not due directly to any wrong moral choice, but is caused by God's decree. Behind all the futility of the world there is God's hope, the confidence which he has in man, and his determination that the universe shall find its perfection only in the perfection of man. Only when man has entered upon his inheritance as son of God can the creation be delivered from its bondage to share in the glory of man's redeemed existence.

Paul never calls Jesus Son of Man, probably because this Semitic title would have been a meaningless barbarism to the Greeks. But he was aware of the primitive tradition in which this title was preserved: he calls Jesus 'the second man' and quotes from the eighth Psalm, with its promise that the glorified Son of Man will have all things put in subjection under his feet.[2] He believes that this glory has already been attained by Christ as 'the Last Adam', the inclusive representative of the humanity that is to be;[3] and as often as a man is baptized into Christ and puts on Christ, there is a καινὴ κτίσις, a renewing of the old creation.[4] But while that which is mortal and corruptible remains, this process of renewal is an inner, hidden process, seen only by the eyes of faith: 'our life is hid with Christ in God.'[5] The Christian has the Spirit as the earnest of his inheritance, and the presence of the

[1] Rom. i. 21. [2] 1 Cor. xv. 47, 25. [3] 1 Cor. xv. 42–45.
[4] 2 Cor. v 17. [5] Col. iii. 3.

Spirit is known by his fruits and by his inner witness that we are sons of God;[1] but for full adoption as a son of God the Christian must await the redemption of the body. The redemption or resurrection of the body is never, in Paul's theology, simply a corporeal but always a corporate event. The body of flesh is the token of man's solidarity in frailty and mortality with all his kind, and indeed with all creation; it is only in this corporate unity, therefore, that he can expect to be redeemed into the new solidarity of the risen body of Christ. 'Our citizenship is in heaven, from whence we await a Saviour, the Lord Jesus Christ, who will transform the body of our humiliation that it may be conformed to the body of his glory.'[2] Thus of all the principalities and powers which must be defeated before the final triumph of God's grace the last enemy is death.[3] While he waits for the conquest of death, the Christian must still groan under the burden of mortality, but his groaning is shared by the whole creation, which watches with breathless expectation for the revealing of the sons of God.

From this magnificent picture of all creation renewed in the renewal of man it is but a small step to Paul's conception of Christ as the first-born of all creation. If creation reaches its perfection only in the perfection of man, and if man's perfection was achieved by Christ, then it follows that when God created the world Christ was his plan and Christ was his purpose. 'In him all things were created, in heaven and on earth, visible and invisible,

[1] Gal. v. 22; Rom. viii. 16.
[2] Phil. iii. 20 f. See also J. A. T. Robinson, *The Body*.
[3] 1 Cor. xv. 26.

whether thrones or dominions or principalities or authorities—all things were created through him and for him.'[1] Upon this divine plan to sum up all things in Christ there had intruded the contradiction of sin; man had come under God's judgement, the heavenly powers had become world-rulers of this darkness, the subhuman creation had been subjected to futility; and all must now be reconciled to God by the blood of the Cross.

[1] Col. i. 16.

What the Rulers Did Not Know

I

THERE is a story told of a former Bishop of Durham that he was accosted one day by a member of the Salvation Army, who asked him: 'Are you saved?' To which the bishop replied: 'That depends on whether you mean σωθείς, σωζόμενος, or σεσωσμένος. If you mean σωθείς, undoubtedly; if you mean σωζόμενος, I trust so; if you mean σεσωσμένος, certainly not'. Σωθείς is an aorist participle, denoting a single act in the past, and it refers either to the finished work of Christ on the Cross or to the baptism in which the Christian has once for all embraced his salvation. Σωζόμενος is a present participle, and describes an ongoing process of salvation, the journey of the Christian from the City of Destruction—or, perhaps we should say, from the Cross, where he felt the burden of sin slip from his shoulders— to the gates of the Celestial City. Σεσωσμένος is a perfect participle, and designates a final consummation, the sounding of the trumpets on the other side, the disclosing of the salvation which is ready to be revealed at the last time. We may, then, paraphrase the bishop's answer as follows: if you mean 'Did Christ die for me?', undoubtedly; if you mean 'Are my feet firmly set upon the highway of salvation?', I trust so; but if you mean 'Am I safe home in the blest kingdoms meek of joy and love?', certainly not.

This story perfectly illustrates the threefold character of the New Testament doctrine of salvation. Salvation in the New Testament is always a past fact, a present experience, and a future hope; and no exposition of New Testament theology is complete which fails to do justice to any of these three aspects. In particular, this threefold character is observable in the passages where Paul speaks of Christ's victory over the powers. In the first chapter I have already drawn attention to the change of attitude towards the powers which Paul underwent in the course of his missionary work. In his earlier letters he speaks only of the defeat of the powers, and if he looks at all beyond defeat it is to their destruction; but in his imprisonment epistles he looks beyond defeat to their reconciliation to God. But whether he is thinking in terms of defeat or of reconciliation, his thought still falls into the same threefold pattern. Christ has won his victory; he has 'disarmed the principalities and authorities . . . triumphing over them in it [sc. the Cross]';[1] he has been exalted 'far above every principality and authority and power and lordship'.[2] Yet the battle still continues, and Christians must still contend 'against the principalities, against the powers, against the world-rulers of this present darkness'.[3] The time between the Resurrection and the Parousia is the reign of Christ, during which he is reducing to impotence 'every principality and every authority and power'. For he must

[1] Col. ii. 15.   [2] Eph. i. 21.   [3] Eph. vi. 12.

reign until he has put all his enemies under his feet'.[1]
Under this continued pressure from the regnant Christ the
powers have become 'the weak and beggarly elemental
spirits',[2] and can be described as 'the rulers of this age
who are being reduced to impotence'.[3] But the final
victory comes only with the Parousia: 'When all things
are subjected to him, then the Son himself also shall be
subjected to him who subjected all things to him, that
God may be all in all.'[4] Again, God has reconciled all
things to himself once for all by the blood of the Cross.[5]
But the process of reconciliation continues through the
ministries of the church: 'God . . . has given to us the
ministry of reconciliation; that is, God in Christ was
reconciling the world to himself.'[6] This ministry of reconciliation is not confined in its scope to humanity, for it is
God's purpose 'that to the principalities and authorities
in the heavenly places there might now be made known
through the church the manifold wisdom of God'.[7] And
the fullness of reconciliation is achieved when God has
worked out his purpose 'to sum up all things in Christ'
($\dot{\alpha}\nu\alpha\kappa\epsilon\phi\alpha\lambda\alpha\iota\dot{\omega}\sigma\alpha\sigma\theta\alpha\iota$ $\tau\dot{\alpha}$ $\pi\dot{\alpha}\nu\tau\alpha$ $\dot{\epsilon}\nu$ $\tau\hat{\omega}$ $X\rho\iota\sigma\tau\hat{\omega}$).[8]

But how is this threefold victory, this threefold reconciliation achieved? In raising this question I am aware
that I am paying my readers a compliment and laying
myself open to a charge of arrogance. For Paul says with
some vehemence that he is prepared to discuss this subject only with the mature. 'We do speak wisdom among
the mature, but a wisdom not of this age nor of the rulers

---

[1] 1 Cor. xv. 24 f. [2] Gal. iv. 9. [3] 1 Cor. ii. 6.
[4] 1 Cor. xv. 28. [5] Col. i. 20. [6] 2 Cor. v. 18 f.
[7] Eph. iii. 10. [8] Eph. i. 10.

of this age who are being reduced to impotence. Rather
do we speak a secret wisdom of God, the hidden wisdom
which God foreordained before the ages for our glory;
which none of the rulers of this age knew; for if they had
known it, they would not have crucified the Lord of
glory.'[1] With this somewhat dark hint Paul turns to deal
with the spiritual qualifications required for those who
are to enter into the mysteries of God, and leaves us to
take our courage in both hands and to ask again, What
was this divine wisdom, this grand strategy of God which
caught the world-rulers off their guard?

To this question Paul's epistles provide no single con-
cise or consistent answer, and this is hardly surprising
when we take account of the extremely complex origins
of his doctrine of principalities and powers. In particular,
the hope that the powers will be reconciled to God is
thrown out without any elaboration, so that we are left
to conjecture what such a hope involves. I think we may
assume, however, that Paul developed his hope of cosmic
reconciliation not as a substitute for his earlier belief in
the defeat of the powers but as its complement, and that
the powers could be reconciled to God only when they
had been deprived of their evil potentiality and made
subject to Christ. I propose, therefore, to leave the idea of
reconciliation on one side, and to concentrate upon the
defeat of the powers. To this end let us select three of the
most striking characteristics of the powers, and see how
they are countered in Paul's gospel of the Cross. Firstly,
then, the powers are subordinate authorities raised to a
position of absolute authority, and they are defeated by

[1] 1 Cor. ii. 6-8.

a revelation of the true nature and purpose of God. Secondly, the powers represent organized evil, evil embedded in the structure of society or woven into the fabric of the universe; and they are defeated by the identification of men with a new organic unity over which evil has no power. Thirdly, the powers owe their hold upon the world and upon humanity in particular to sin, and they are defeated by the unyielding obedience of Christ.

Let us begin by examining Paul's belief in *victory through revelation*.

II

'The god of this age has blinded the minds of the unbelieving.'[1] Spiritual blindness is the fate which overtakes all who worship that which is not God, or devote their wholehearted allegiance to a cause other than God's eternal purpose of grace. The nationalist is blind to anything but the supremacy of his own people. The legalist is blind to anything except his own standards of righteousness. The determinist is blind to anything except the suffocating reign of causality. In his utter devotion to the law Paul had experienced that blindness, a blindness which had even driven him to persecute the Son of God. Then he became aware that in Christ God had revealed himself not as justice but as love. 'God commended his love towards us in that while we were yet sinners Christ died for us.'[2] This revelation was an objective fact; it happened at a datable point in history. But it came home to Paul as an inner experience: 'It pleased God to reveal

[1] 2 Cor. iv. 4.   [2] Rom. v. 8.

his Son in me.'[1] Only by such an experience, which healed the blindness of his inner eye, could the historic fact become visible to him.

Paul speaks of his conversion as the taking away of a veil from his heart, and he believed that whenever a man turned to the Lord in faith a similar veil of misunderstanding was removed.[2] He speaks of it as an illumination, in which he saw the glory of God accurately mirrored in Christ, the image of God.[3] In his later epistles he speaks also of the disclosure of the hidden mystery of God, the publication of God's secret plan of redemption.[4] But we must not allow such expressions to mislead us into thinking that for Paul revelation meant simply a new conception of God. It was God himself who had been revealed in all his saving power. The righteousness of God which was revealed in the Gospel was not merely a divine quality but a divine activity.[5] The glory of God which Paul saw in the face of Jesus Christ was the glory of the Creator engaged in a new act of creation. 'God who commanded light to shine out of darkness has shined in our hearts to give the illumination of the knowledge of the glory of God in the face of Jesus Christ.'[6]

As a result of this access of divine glory the powers were shown up as usurpers of the divine majesty and impostors in the claims which they made upon man's allegiance. Paul has a remarkable range of imagery with which to describe the exposure of the tyrants who had so long held humanity in bondage. In an almost untranslatable

[1] Gal. i. 16.   [2] 2 Cor. iii. 16.
[3] 2 Cor. iv. 4, 6; cf. Eph. i. 18; ii. 9; 2 Tim. i. 10; Heb. vi. 4, 32.
[4] Col. i. 26; Eph. iii. 3–5.   [5] Rom. i. 17.   [6] 2 Cor. iv. 6.

sentence in 2 Corinthians he declares that the old covenant, the transient dispensation of death and condemnation, which embodies a measure of the divine glory, has
been 'deglorified' by reason of the superlative glory of
the new convenant in Christ.[1] In the light of this glory
the powers now appear as 'weak and beggarly elemental
spirits'.[2] Like a Roman emperor, entering the capital in
triumphal procession with a train of discredited enemies
behind the chariot, Christ has made an exhibition of the
powers, celebrating a public triumph over them.[3] These
extravagant terms do not mean that Paul had any illu-
sions about the strength of the spiritual forces with which
he and his fellow Christians must yet do battle. But they
do mean that Paul had seen the principalities and powers
for the first time in their true guise, and that for him all
such influences had sunk into insignificance before the
vision of an invincible love, from which henceforth nothing in all creation would be able to separate him.

God had revealed himself once and for all in Christ; he
had revealed himself personally to Paul; and, as often as
a man turned to the Lord, this personal revelation would
be repeated. But besides the initial experience of illumination at conversion Paul seems to have believed in a continuing revelation through the work of the indwelling
Spirit.

As it is written, 'Things which eye has not seen, nor ear
heard, nor the heart of man conceived, things which God has
prepared for those who love him', God has revealed to us
through the Spirit. For the Spirit searches all things, even the
depths of God. For what man knows a man's thoughts except

[1] 2 Cor. iii. 10.　　　　[2] Gal. iv. 9.　　　　[3] Col. ii. 15.

the man's spirit that is in him? So too no one knows God's thoughts except the Spirit of God. Now we have not received the spirit of the world but the Spirit which comes from God, that we may know the gifts bestowed on us by God.[1]

This does not mean that anything needs to be added to the historic revelation of Christ. In Christ God's 'whole name appears complete'; but man's appropriation and understanding of that revelation is a slow and lengthy process, which begins at conversion and continues throughout life, a process which can be achieved only under the guidance of the interpreter Spirit. This passage follows immediately upon Paul's mention of 'the rulers of this age who are being reduced to impotence', and suggests strongly that the continuing defeat of the rulers depends on the continuing revelation of God through the Spirit.

There remained, however, a further revelation for which Paul waited with expectancy. Like other New Testament writers he sometimes described the Parousia as the revelation or manifestation of Christ.[2] But for Paul this was not to be just the return of him who since his Ascension had been hidden from sight and known only to faith; it was to be the point when those who had been united with Christ in his suffering would be united with him also in his glory.[3] For the glory of God must be revealed not only in Christ, the Son of God, but also in all those who through Christ enter upon the life of sonship. Already the process has begun: 'we all, with unveiled face reflecting the glory of the Lord, are

[1] 1 Cor. ii. 9–12.   [2] 1 Cor. i. 7; 2 Thess. i. 7; ii. 8.
[3] Rom. viii. 17.

being transformed into the same image from glory to glory, through the action of the Lord the Spirit.'[1] But it is a hidden process, concealed beneath man's outer garment of mortality, and brought to its completion only with the redemption of the body. 'Your life is hid with Christ in God; when Christ, your life, shall appear, then you also shall appear with him in glory.'[2] It is to this final revelation of Christ, not in the individual glory of his risen life but in the corporate resurrection of his body which is the church, that Paul sees the final defeat of the powers. When all that is mortal has put on immortality, then Death, the last enemy, shall be swallowed up in victory.[3] And when men stand revealed as sons of God, then the creation too may be set free from the bondage of decay to share in the liberty of their glory.[4]

This final triumph, however, involves some kind of identification of the Christian with Christ, and so we turn in the second place to *victory through identification.*

III

We have long been familiar with what H. W. Robinson has called 'corporate personality'—the principle whereby the group may be treated as a unit for purposes of law or religion. But for the Pauline doctrine of redemption it is important to recognize that there are two types of corporate unity, the natural and the voluntary. Natural unity is seen in the family or tribe: they belong together by what we call blood-relationship, and what the Old Testament calls bone and flesh. 'We are your bone and

[1] 2 Cor. iii. 18.   [2] Col. iii. 3 f.
[3] 1 Cor. xv. 54.   [4] Rom. viii. 21.

your flesh',[1] say the tribes of Israel to David when they come to make him king. In the eyes of God they belong together, too, both for good and for evil: he 'keeps faith with families . . . and visits the iniquity of the fathers upon the children',[2] because family solidarity is a fact of the religious life. But such solidarity can be produced also by voluntary action. 'Whither you go I will go', says Ruth to Naomi, 'and where you lodge I will lodge: your people shall be my people, and your God my God: where you die I will die, and there will I be buried.'[3] Old Testament law provided that the resident foreigner could become naturalized as a *ger* or proselyte, and the presence of these *gerim* was a constant reminder to Israel that her relationship to Yahweh was based on a covenant and not on natural descent. The native Israelite and the *ger* were both alike in this respect, that they belonged to the people of God by an act of grace. Thus it could sometimes be said that all Israelites were equally Yahweh's *gerim*.[4]

The perfect human example of this voluntary solidarity is the marriage covenant, in which by contract man and woman become 'one flesh'. How complete this identification could be is illustrated by the story of Abigail. Her husband Nabal had offered a gratuitous insult to David, who was threatening summary vengeance; and Abigail, though herself innocent, was prepared to make herself accountable for her husband's misdoings: 'Upon me, my lord, upon me be the iniquity.'[5]

A large part of Paul's theology is concerned with the

---

[1] 2 Sam. v. 1.   [2] Exod. xxxiv. 7.   [3] Ruth i. 16 f.
[4] Lev. xxv. 23; Ps. xxxix. 12; cxix. 19; 1 Chr. xxix. 15.
[5] 1 Sam. xxv. 24.

transference of men from a natural unity to a voluntary one, from the solidarity of nature to the solidarity of grace, from Adam to Christ. By Adam Paul means not simply the first man but the natural corporate unity of the human race, in which all men are indissolubly united by their common participation in the body of flesh. This flesh is not in itself sinful, but it is the means by which sin spreads its effects throughout the body of humanity. These effects are twofold, for men are related to the sin of Adam in two distinct ways—by implication and by imitation. Within any corporate unity men are implicated in the corporate sin, whether or not they have consented to the commission of it. In a nation, for instance, every citizen is involved in national sin. So in the larger unit of humanity all men are implicated in the common sin, which had its origin in Adam's disobedience, and therefore all have come under the reign of sin and death, which is the wages of sin. But Paul is careful to add that all men have contributed to the corporate sin of humanity, inasmuch as all have sinned after the pattern of Adam's transgression.[1] This double relationship of the natural man to sin carries with it also a double relationship to the flesh. To be in the flesh means to belong to the corporate unit of humanity within which the unredeemed passions and impulses of men wreak their fearful consequences. But to do the works of the flesh,[2] to have the mind of the flesh,[3] to allow sin to reign in one's mortal body,[4] is to participate actively in the general sinfulness.

We are now in a position to appreciate the blunder

[1] Rom. v. 12–14.   [2] Gal. v. 19.
[3] Rom. viii. 5 f.   [4] Rom. vi. 12.

which the rulers of this age committed when they crucified the Lord of Glory. The control which they exercised
over human life was the result of the universality of sin,
and they claimed control over Christ because he too was
a man. What they did not realize was that Christ belonged
to the corporate unity of mankind not by nature but by
his own free choice. He had chosen to be 'found in fashion
as a man'.[1] It was through 'the grace of the Lord Jesus
Christ that though he was rich yet for our sakes he became
poor, that we through his poverty might become rich'.[2]
Paul leaves it in no doubt that Christ's self-identification
with sinful humanity was complete, that he was Very
Man. 'God sent his own Son in the likeness of sinful
flesh.'[3] 'He has made him to be sin for us, who knew no
sin.'[4] 'Christ has redeemed us from the curse of the law,
being made a curse for us.'[5] By his own voluntary act he
made himself accountable for the common sins of men,
and so submitted to the reign of death. But because his
involvement was voluntary, because he identified himself
with sinful humanity without actually committing sin,
death could never be for him what it was for the sinner.
Sin separates man from God, and death is the final
separation, the final defeat. But for him who knew no
sin, death had exactly the opposite effect. As long as he
was in the flesh he was subject to temptation, and the
possibility remained that he might do the works of the
flesh, and so allow sin to reign in his mortal body; but
with the death of the flesh that possibility no longer
existed. Thus in putting Christ to death the powers were

[1] Phil. ii. 8.   [2] 2 Cor. viii. 8.   [3] Rom. viii. 3.
[4] 2 Cor. v. 21.   [5] Gal. iii. 13.

not asserting their control over him, they were losing the only chance of control they ever had, 'For he that is dead is freed from sin.'[1]

The Cross, then, was a personal victory for Christ which carried him beyond the dominion of the powers; by liberating him from the body of flesh it enabled him also to 'disarm the principalities and authorities',[2] to take from them the only weapon they could ever use against him. But the Cross was also a corporate victory. By identifying himself with men in their sinfulness and humiliation Christ had made it possible for men to be identified with him in his righteousness and triumph. He had become the Last Adam, the head of a new humanity, and in him all mankind had passed vicariously through death and resurrection into a new life over which the principalities and powers had no control. 'If we have died with Christ, we believe that we shall also live with him: knowing that Christ being raised from the dead dies no more; death has no more dominion over him.'[3] The rulers of this age would not have crucified the Lord of Glory if they had known that in so doing they were not gaining control over Christ but losing control over all men.

The one condition of participation in this new humanity is faith, and we may define faith as a wholehearted acceptance of identification with Christ. Men belong to Adam by nature but to Christ by consent; and as Christ chose to be identified with sinful men, so they must choose to be identified with him. The new corporate humanity of Christ is an objective reality which becomes

[1] Rom. vi. 7.   [2] Col. ii. 15.
[3] Rom. vi. 8–9.

a fact of experience only through faith.[1] But the Christ of faith is still the crucified and risen Lord, and to be identified with him is to be united with him in death and resurrection. At the outset of the Christian life this death of the old nature and its resurrection into the new manhood of Christ is sacramentally represented by baptism. 'For all we who have been baptized into Christ have put on Christ. . . . And those who belong to Christ Jesus have crucified the flesh with its passions and lusts.'[2] 'Do you not know that all we who were baptized into Christ Jesus were baptized into his death? We were buried with him, therefore, through baptism unto death, that as Christ was raised from the dead by the glory of the Father, so also we might walk in newness of life. For if we have become grafted into him in the likeness of his death, so shall we also be in the likeness of his resurrection.'[3] Baptism, therefore, signifies the Christian's initial victory over the powers of evil. 'You have died with Christ *out from under* the elemental spirits of the world.'[4] 'Thanks be to God who gives us the victory through our Lord Jesus Christ.'[5]

Up to this point we have been discussing the Christian's identification with Christ as a past fact, achieved through the Incarnation and, above all, through the Cross, and appropriated in baptism by those who have put their faith in Christ. But the victory which comes to Christians at baptism as a gift from God through Christ crucified must

[1] Cf. 1 Jn. v. 4: 'This is the victory that overcomes the world, our faith.'   [2] Gal. iii. 27; v. 24.

[3] Rom. vi. 3–5.

[4] Col. ii. 20; I owe this translation to J. A. T. Robinson, op. cit., p. 43.

[5] 1 Cor. xv. 57.

be worked out in the continuous experience of the Christian life. Having died to sin at baptism they must continually reckon themselves dead to sin.[1] They must 'put to death the deeds of the body'.[2] The putting on of Christ is also a continuous process which involves the habitual ordering of daily life by the new ethical standards of the Gospel. 'Seeing that you have put off the old manhood with its deeds, and have put on the new . . . put on, therefore, as elect of God, holy and beloved, a heart of compassion, kindness, humility of mind, meekness, long-suffering: forbearing one another and forgiving one another, if any man has a quarrel against another: as Christ forgave you, so also do you. And above all these things put on love which is the bond of perfection.'[3] In writing to his friends in Philippi Paul refers in moving language to his own unremitting efforts to live out from day to day the implications of his baptism.

For his sake I have suffered the loss of all things, and count them as refuse, that I may gain Christ . . . that I may know him and the power of his resurrection and the fellowship of his suffering, being conformed to his death, if perchance I may attain the resurrection from the dead. Not that I have already obtained or am already perfected; but I press on to make it my own, inasmuch as Christ Jesus has also made me his own.[4]

The relation between this aspect of the Christian life and the reign of the principalities and powers is made abundantly clear in the Epistle to the Galatians. There, it will be remembered, Paul declares that Jew and Gentile

[1] Rom. vi. 11.
[2] Rom. viii. 13.
[3] Col. iii. 9–14.
[4] Phil. iii. 8–12.

alike have lived under the elemental spirits of this world and that for both alike this reign has been a reign of law. Those who have been baptized into Christ and have put on Christ have been delivered from this bondage. Now it appears that there were in Galatia Judaizers who wished to impose the Torah or parts of it upon their fellow Christians, in the belief that such a discipline would bring them to religious maturity. Paul addresses this group three times. 'Why do you turn back again to the weak and beggarly elements, to which you want to be enslaved all over again?'[1] 'Tell me, you who want to be under law, do you not listen to the law?'[2] 'You are severed from Christ, you who would be justified by the law; you have fallen away from grace.'[3] The Christian must choose between the dominion of the elemental spirits and the dominion of Christ, and those who voluntarily re-enter the one are thereby severing their connexion with the other. Paul's contention was that the Christian life must be lived not by the rules of any legal code but by the guidance of the Spirit; and 'where the Spirit of the Lord is there is liberty'.[4] It is in the exercise of this Christian freedom that men can demonstrate the victory which Christ has won for them over the principalities and powers. 'For freedom Christ has set us free: stand fast, therefore, and be not entangled again in a yoke of bondage.'[5]

But the full liberty and the final victory remain as a hope for the future. The identification of Christians with

[1] Gal. iv. 9.
[2] Gal. iv. 21.
[3] Gal. v. 4.
[4] 2 Cor. iii. 17.
[5] Gal. v. 1.

Christ is a process which can be complete only when all things are summed up in Christ. Paul's experience as 'a man in Christ' led him to repudiate the narrow particularism of Jewish orthodoxy and to embrace a larger hope. If Paul, the flagrant sinner who had persecuted the church of God, could be united with Christ, then no limits could be placed to the redeeming power of victorious love. Christ had died for all and so had become the Last Adam, whose triumph would be complete only when all mankind had come to participate in his risen life. Even the disaffection of the greater part of his own nation could not dim his confidence. The setting aside of the Jews was only a temporary measure whereby God had provided for the ingrafting of the Gentiles into Christ. 'A partial hardening has come upon Israel, until the fulness of the Gentiles comes in, and then all Israel shall be saved. . . . For God has shut up all men into disobedience that he may have mercy upon all.'[1] Thus Paul looked forward to the time when the victory of God, achieved in the representative death and resurrection of Christ, and effective wherever the gift of divine grace was accepted by faith, would reach its culmination in a world redeemed.

But we have not yet penetrated deeply enough into the divine wisdom. The defeat of the powers through the identification of Christians with Christ depends on one fundamental condition—that Christ himself was without sin so that the powers never had any real hold on him. We turn, therefore, in the third place to *victory through obedience.*

[1] Rom. xi. 25, 32.

IV

'As by one man's disobedience many were made sinners, so by the obedience of one shall many be made righteous.'[1] It is because men are sinners that the powers exercise dominion over them, and the transforming of sinners into righteous men is the final defeat of the powers. This point is set out in greater detail in Paul's famous hymn on the Incarnation.

He took the form of a slave, being born in the likeness of men. And being found in human form he humbled himself, becoming obedient unto death, even death on a cross. Therefore God has also highly exalted him and has given him the name which is above every name, that at the name of Jesus every knee should bow, of those in heaven and those on earth and those under the earth, and that every tongue should confess that Jesus Christ is Lord to the glory of God the Father.[2]

In the last analysis it is to the obedience of Jesus that the powers in heaven, along with all other creatures, must bow the knee. It is of the greatest importance in expounding this passage that we should observe the order of the clauses. Paul does not say that Christ became man, and then chose from among other human possibilities to adopt the rank of a slave. 'He took the form of a slave, being born in the likeness of men.' The servile form was an unavoidable part of the human nature which he assumed. All men are born slaves, born into the general servitude to the powers of this present age. This bondage Christ accepted for himself in becoming man. But unlike

[1] Rom. v. 19. [2] Phil. ii. 7–11.

other men he was able to absorb all that the powers could do to him and to neutralize it by his unwavering obedience to God. And herein lay his victory.

Evil propagates itself by a chain reaction. It is like a bad coin, which is passed on from one person to another until it reaches someone who will put it out of currency by absorbing the loss. If one man injures another, there are three ways in which evil can win a victory and only one way in which it can be defeated. If the injured person retaliates, or nurses a grievance, or takes it out on a third person, the evil is perpetuated and is therefore victorious. Evil is defeated only if the injured person absorbs the evil and refuses to allow it to go any farther. It is this kind of victory which Paul describes when he says that Christ 'died to sin'.[1] Without doing anything to perpetuate evil, he submitted to all that sin could do to him until death carried him beyond its power. But he did more than this: 'he died for our sins.'[2] He drew off on to himself the evil effects of other men's sins; he faced the powers of evil and drew their fire.

Two examples will suffice to show that this gospel of the Cross is not only theologically true but is also an historically true account of the ministry of Jesus. One of the reasons why the Pharisees broke with Jesus was that he was the 'friend of publicans and sinners'. Because he deliberately set himself to make common cause with the outcast and the downtrodden, the law-abiding Jews repudiated him as a breaker of the law. He drew off on to himself all the contempt and hostility which the respectable were prepared to heap upon their less virtuous

[1] Rom. v. 10.   [2] 1 Cor. xv. 3.

brethren. Similarly, when he went into the temple and expelled the traders from the court of the Gentiles, reminding them of the Scripture which said, 'My house shall be a house of prayer for all nations', he was drawing off on to himself all the accumulated enmity which down the centuries had separated Jew and Gentile. It was this chosen path that led him to the Cross. But with what results? 'He is our peace, who has made us both one, and has broken down the dividing wall, the hostility, by abolishing in his flesh the law of commandments with its legal demands, that he might create in himself one new man in the place of the two, so making peace, and might reconcile us both to God in one body through the cross, having slain the hostility in it.'[1] By drawing off on to himself the hostility with which men regarded one another, and by allowing it to put him on the Cross, he has slain the hostility. But it should be noted that the hostility between Pharisee and sinner and between Jew and Gentile was an inevitable consequence of the tyranny of the law. The slaying of the hostility involved the abolition of the law, and so constituted a victory over the angelic guardians of legal religion.

The victory does not stop there, for the obedience of Christ must be reproduced in the lives of his followers. 'Let this mind be in you which was also in Christ Jesus, who . . . humbled himself, becoming obedient unto death.'[2] We must be careful not to misstate this part of Paul's teaching. Paul repeatedly and indignantly rejects the idea that by our own obedience to God's commands we may achieve a victory over the powers of evil. It is

[1] Eph. ii. 14–16. [2] Phil. ii. 5 ff.

'God who gives us the victory through our Lord Jesus Christ.'[1] 'It is Christ Jesus who died, yea, who was raised from the dead, who is at the right hand of God, who also intercedes for us.'[2] It is the Spirit of life in Christ who sets us free from the law of sin and death.[3] But in setting us free Christ bestows upon us a new life, a new life which is his own life, and which is therefore a life of obedience. It follows, then, that Christ's method of dealing with evil must be our method also. As 'men in Christ' we must be ready to absorb all that the powers of evil can do to us, and to neutralize it with forgiving love. 'Be not outwardly conformed to this age, but be transformed by the renewing of your mind. . . . Recompense to no man evil for evil. . . . Avenge not yourselves but give place to wrath. . . . If your enemy is hungry, feed him; if he is thirsty, give him drink. . . . Do not be overcome by evil, but overcome evil with good.'[4] Any other method of meeting evil means being conformed to this present age, which is under the domination of the principalities and powers. Any other method of meeting evil means being severed from Christ. Any other method of meeting evil is a reversion to the weak and beggarly elements from whose bondage Christ has set us free.

This may seem to be a high standard, but Paul is bold enough to point to his own life as an illustration of his doctrine. 'I rejoice in my sufferings for your sake, and in my flesh I fill up for my part that which is lacking of the afflictions of Christ on behalf of his body, which is the church.'[5] Paul is not saying here that there was anything

[1] 1 Cor. xv. 57.   [2] Rom. viii. 34.   [3] Rom. viii. 2.
[4] Rom. xii.   [5] Col. i. 24.

incomplete about Christ's atoning work. He means that because the life of the church is Christ's own life, it is of necessity a life of suffering; and he trusts that his life, filled as it is with multifarious afflictions, has served to draw off from his Christian brethren something of the load of suffering which would otherwise have been theirs.

The powers of evil have been defeated by the obedience of Christ; they are constantly being defeated whenever Christians face them in the panoply of God; but the final triumph comes only when divine love has absorbed the whole momentum of evil, drawn its last sting, neutralized its full effects. We have already seen that this final triumph is to be the revelation of God's glory, reproduced in the sons of God, that it is to be the summing up of all things in Christ. Now there remains one more thing to be said.

I have tried in these pages to expound Paul's view of man's dilemma, that he lives under divinely appointed authorities—the powers of state, the powers of legal religion, the powers of nature—which through sin have become demonic agencies. To expect that evil will be defeated by any of these powers, by the action of state, by the self-discipline of the conscience, or by the processes of nature, is to ask that Satan cast out Satan. The powers can be robbed of their tyrannical influence and brought into their proper subjection to God only in the Cross. The final victory, then, is the Parousia of him who once was crucified; and that means that when God pronounces his last word in the drama of this world's redemption, he will vindicate the way of the Cross, and he will vindicate nothing else.

INDEX LOCORUM

PRINTED IN
GREAT BRITAIN
AT THE
UNIVERSITY PRESS
OXFORD
BY
CHARLES BATEY
PRINTER
TO THE
UNIVERSITY